W9-BUL-889

# America Balkanized

# Balkanized

Immigration's Challenge to Government

by
Brent A. Nelson

# America Balkanized

Immigration's Challenge to Government

by
Brent A. Nelson, Ph.D.

The American Immigration Control Foundation
Monterey, Virginia

The American Immigration Control Foundation is a non-
partisan, non-profit public policy research
organization. The analyses, conclusions, and opinions
expressed in its publications are those of the authors
and not necessarily those of the Foundation, or of its
officers, directors, or others associated with, or
funding, its work.


Inquiries, book orders, and catalog requests
should be addressed to

AICF
Post Office Box 525
Monterey, Virginia 24465.


Library of Congress Cataloging-in-Publication Data:

Nelson, Brent A.
   America balkanized: immigration's challenge to
government / by Brent A. Nelson
   Includes bibliographical references.
   ISBN 0-936247-14-2 : $10.00
   1. United States--Emigration and immigration--
Government policy. 2. United States--Emigration and
immigration. 3. United States--Ethnic relations.
I. Title.
JV6493.N45 1994
304.8'2'0973--dc20                              94-4306
                                                  CIP

# Contents

# *Foreword*

*America Balkanized* is an essay in social criticism, a contribution to the ongoing debate regarding immigration. It is an essay in the sense that it is merely an attempt to examine some aspects of a multi-faceted subject; i.e., the problems of governance in the multi-ethnic state which will arise in the United States if immigration is not curtailed. Although its argument draws upon scholarship, cited in the notes, the essay does not presume to examine its topic from the stance of value-free scholarship. Rather, it is based upon definite judgments of value regarding public policy, government, and nationhood.

The public policy of a nation should promote the welfare of those who are citizens of the nation, either native or naturalized, before that of all other peoples in the world. Other peoples should be the concern only of that nation's foreign policy and only insofar as relations with them affect the welfare of the nation's citizens. Furthermore, the welfare of the citizens of a nation is not promoted when citizens of other nations are invited into the nation to partake of economic goods and natural resources which are becoming increasingly limited within that nation.

The government of a nation is confronted with a serious challenge when new entrants become part of one or more political blocs arising not from differences regarding governmental philosophy but merely from differences of ethnic origin. The mobilization of ethnic blocs as political conflict groups during an era of declining economic expectations will present a government with a growing problem of conflict management. A government obliged to contend with chronic conflict will become an increasingly costly and intrusive government. When conflicts are deeply rooted, long continued, and have a basis in fundamental ethnic divisions, they can threaten the very political integrity of the nation itself.

If a nation is to endure, it must be based upon something more vital, and less ephemeral, than lines drawn upon a map. The annals of history and the new science of sociobiology both indicate that nationhood is sustained by a continuity of ethnic descent, and the sense of fellow-feeling arising therefrom, which cannot be conjured into being by the mere will of politicians. There is no reason to believe that the United States will prove to be an exception to the laws of history and nature. Immigration out of control has the potential to destroy American nationhood. If trends apparent during the 1990s continue, the future Balkanization of America is a very real possibility.

Finally, let it not be assumed that *America Balkanized* has been written to advance the agenda of groups at either end of the political spectrum. The conclusion, "The Outlook for America," offers a critical assessment of the arguments and motivations of opponents of immigration control who represent both the right and the left. Exponents of *laissez-faire* and of "multiculturalism" advocate "open borders" for divergent reasons, but both agree in giving American national survival a low place on their lists of priorities. Immigration control is essential if America is to preserve its "vital center" and, with that, its nationhood.

# I

# *An Influx of Immigrants*

During the 1980s, several observers of political trends in the United States warned that the growing Spanish-speaking population in the Southwest might one day pose a challenge to national unity similar to that presented by the French-speaking population in Canada. The best known among them, Richard D. Lamm, a former governor of Colorado, wrote in 1986 that "I am concerned about the danger of countries in which two language groups clash. I think about the problems caused by Quebec's separatist movement, founded upon the French language. I think about the tensions even within peaceful multilingual countries: the cantonization of Switzerland and the division of Belgium."[1] Writing in 1987, former Senator Eugene McCarthy warned of a "recolonization" which has one manifestation in "the challenge to the status of English in the United States. There has been both a practical and a legal submission to demands that at least some parts of the country should become bilingual or multilingual."[2]

The concerns of Governor Lamm and Senator McCarthy had been expressed earlier by two respected scholars. Victor Ferkiss, a noted historian of American politics, wrote in 1980 that "Current American legal doctrine and ethnic political pressures have created a situation where all of the political and cultural problems of bilingualism that have riven Canada are beginning to arise in the United States, especially in the Southwest."[3] George Fredrickson, a prominent historian of race relations, offered the following observations at a colloquium in 1982:

> I think what's likely to be the most difficult problem in 30 or 40 years is the question of the relation between Mexican-Americans or Chicanos and whites. Remember that we stole the Southwest from Mexico once. There are two ways

1

that you can gain territory from another country. One is by conquest. That's essentially the way we took California from Mexico and, in a sense, Texas as well, . . . But what's going on now may end up being a kind of recolonization of the Southwest, because the other way you can regain territory is by population infiltration and demographic dominance . . . . The United States will be faced with the problem that Canada has been faced with . . . and which our system is not prepared to accommodate.[4]

Noting that the mass media gave little attention to their warnings, skeptics have dismissed Lamm, McCarthy, Ferkiss, and Fredrickson as prophets of doom, haunted by the spectre of a "Hispanic Quebec" which will never become a reality. According to this popular interpretation of the problem, it will remain problematic for only a limited period of time. Millions of immigrants have entered the U.S. in past decades, according to this reassuring argument, and have been more or less readily assimilated into the mainstream of American social and political life.

This optimistic assessment overlooks, however, the transforming impact of a significant change in the origins of the region's population combined with an ongoing failure of the process of assimilation. The demographic shift in the Southwest resulting from an influx of immigrants and differential birthrates among different elements of the population is, going into the 1990s, increasingly evident. The decline of the assimilative powers of American society, while not so evident, can be inferred from the experience of numerous other societies and becomes increasingly apparent within the U.S. itself. Both factors converge to make more and more probable, if not inevitable, the rise of ethnic separatism within the American Southwest and elsewhere.

The demographic factor alone, assuming continued immigration, could transform the Southwest into a "Hispanic Quebec" long before the close of the twenty-first century. According to the rather conservative estimates of demographers Leon F. Bouvier and Cary B. Davis in their *Immigration and the Future Racial Composition of the United States,* Hispanics, over half of whom are or will be Mexican Americans, will comprise 34.1 percent of the total population of the U.S. in 2080, even if the U.S. limits immigration to two million entrants each year from all areas of the world while birthrates of Hispanics converge with those of non-Hispanics, a possibly unrealistic assumption.[5] Though 34.1 percent is less than a majority of the total population of the U.S., its impact will be overwhelming in the Southwest, where Hispanics will constitute a majority of the population in several states.

Bouvier and Davis also provide estimates of the Hispanic percentages of the populations of California and Texas in 2080, based on a lower estimate of one million immigrants annually. These estimates reveal that Hispanics, at 41.1 percent of California's population and 53.5 percent of Texas's, will constitute either a plurality or a majority of those states' populations.[6] Comparable estimates for the two states, based on an annual immigration total of two million, yield Hispanic percentages in 2040 of, respectively, 42.9 and 52.3.[7]

Not all immigrants, of course, will be Hispanics. Bouvier and Davis, on the basis of an annual immigration total of one million, project a striking rise in the percentage of Californians who are "Asian and Other," from 6.6 percent in 1980 to 18.7 percent in 2040. The comparable estimates for Texans are 1.4 and 5.7 percent.[8] The rise in both states of large blocs of non-Hispanic immigrants will further divide the states culturally and politically, enhancing the relative electoral weight of a well-organized and ethnically conscious Hispanic plurality. Hispanic voting blocs of 40 to 50 percent of the electorate, which, in accord with these most conservative demographic estimates, can be projected for these states in 2080, would suffice to control an electoral process in which the remainder of the electorate would be divided among at least two to three major ethnic blocs.

Working as scientists, Bouvier and Davis have given all possible weight to variables, such as the convergence of the birthrates of all racial groups, that would tend to militate against their thesis that even low levels of immigration, given the origin of most immigrants from Third World nations, will transform the racial composition of the nation's population. Their estimates, therefore, represent, if anything, conservative understatements of the extent of such a transformation.

Given their essentially conservative methodology, Bouvier and Davis have not taken account of a factor that is likely to accelerate the demographic transformation of the Southwest. This is the probability that non-Hispanic whites will move from the Southwest, abandoning areas of it to Hispanics, much as they began in the 1980s to abandon areas of southern Florida. According to an article in the May 3, 1987, issue of the *Miami Herald*, "Despite a near-doubling of the population since 1960, fewer non-Hispanic whites live in Dade [county] now. They have declined from 80 percent of the population to 37 percent."[9] The article quotes Anthony La Greca, director of the Urban Research Center at the University of Florida, as saying, in the words of the *Herald's* staff reporter, that "The sheer concentration of Hispanics in Dade has made non-Hispanic white flight virtually inevitable . . . . [A] tipping point" occurs "when the new ethnic group rises to between 15 and 30 percent of a neighborhood's population."[10] The 1990 U.S. Census of Dade County reported that non-Hispanic whites had further declined to the level of 30.2 percent, while Hispanics had, at 49.2 percent, almost become a majority of the county's population.[11]

There is some evidence suggesting that "white flight" from Southern California had begun by the beginning of the 1980s. According to a preliminary report of the Urban Institute, *The Fourth Wave: California's Newest*

*Immigrants,* published in 1984, "During the 1970s, Southern California experienced, no doubt for the first time since the mid-nineteenth century, a small net outflow of native-born persons."[12] While 886,000 foreign-born persons entered Los Angeles County during the 1970s, more than one million native-born persons left as part of a population shift which resulted in the net gain for Southern California of 1,266,000 foreign-born and a net loss for the area of 223,000 native-born.[13] According to a 1984 report by the Southern California Association of Governments, "Between 1970 and 1980, the Hispanic population in Southern California doubled to 2.8 million . . . the Asian population more than tripled while the number of whites -- excluding Hispanics -- declined by 500,000. By the year 2000, the report predicted, 42 percent of Southern California's residents will be Caucasian, 41 percent Hispanic, 9 percent Asian and 8 percent black."[14]

Writing toward the end of 1989 in the *New York Times,* Robert Reinhold's look at Los Angeles referred to ". . . powerful social and economic changes sweeping the nation's second largest greater metropolitan area, after New York. Many middle-class whites are abandoning the region to those who can afford $500,000 or more for ordinary homes, to impoverished, unskilled Hispanic immigrants, to poor blacks for the most part left out of the surging economy, and to a new wave of entrepreneurial Asians."[15] As a result, Reinhold reported, "some experts say,. . . the six counties centering on the city are becoming a land of rich and poor, with few people in between -- like a Third World country. 'Two cultures are growing up totally diametrically opposed to each other -- social dynamite is building,' said David G. Shulman, an economist formerly with the University of California at Los Angeles Business Forecasting Project."[16]

Occasionally, reporters surveying the Southern California scene suggest that lower-income whites in particular have begun to vacate the area. Thus, Jay Mathews, writing in the *Washington Post* in 1988, noted that "Mostly gone from eastern Los Angeles are the blue-collar Anglo immigrants from Europe and the American South . . . ."[17] Thomas Muller, author of the Urban Institute study, writing on "Economic Effects of Immigration" in *Clamor at the Gates: The New American Immigration,* noted that "During the 1970s, about 250,000 persons with a college education came to California from other states, while close to 100,000 with little education left, a pattern also observed in the early 1980s."[18]

It may not be too melodramatic to suggest that in the twenty-first century there will be a reversal of the migration patterns of the 1930s, in which "poor whites" will flee California rather than seek to enter it as an economic Promised Land. There is impressionistic evidence that some working class citizens in Southern California had, during the 1980s, begun to suffer an extreme degree of immiseration solely due to the alien influx. C.C. Bruno, for example, begins his poignant account of "Why I Am Homeless," which appeared in the May-June 1989 issue of *The Humanist,* with the flat assertion that "In 1986, I joined the ranks of the homeless, forced there by the influx of the new and younger agricultural workers admitted to the United States under the Immigration and Naturalization Reform Act of 1986."[19]

Added to this pattern of "white flight," just in its incipient stages at the beginning of the 1990s, is the factor of differential birthrates among population groups. Kevin McCarthy, a demographic expert with the RAND Corporation, interviewed by the *San Jose Mercury News* in 1987, noted that the recent increase in births in California was a direct consequence of immigration: "In Los Angeles, the figures I've seen are that 80 percent of the natural increase is among Latinos and Asians . . . . So it's not so much a resurgence of Anglos having babies as it is a byproduct of rapid immigration among people whose fertility is higher than Anglos."[20] This demographic wave of the future became even more apparent in California's public schools in the fall of 1988, when non-Hispanic whites became a minority of students enrolled. At that time, non-Hispanic whites were already a minority of 47 percent in the public schools of New Mexico and, at 51.8 percent, were projected to be only two years away from becoming a minority among students enrolled in the public schools in Texas.[21] California's state superintendent of schools reported then that 600,000 students were enrolled in bilingual education programs.[22]

The demographic transformation that became increasingly apparent in Southern California during the 1980s also became evident in southern Texas. According to a report on the population of Texas, prepared in 1986 by demographers at Texas A & M University, several counties of the Coastal Bend Council of Governments had majorities of Hispanics in their populations. These included the populous county of Nueces (which has Corpus Christi as its county seat) and the other counties of Brooks, Duval, Jim Wells, and Kleberg. The counties of Bee, Refugio, and San Patricio had Hispanic populations that were almost a majority of their total populations.[23] San Antonio, next to Houston the largest city in south Texas and the ninth-largest city in the U.S., had in 1986 a majority of Hispanics in its population,[24] as did El Paso, where 71 percent of the first-grade school children were Hispanics.[25]

Although Houston, fourth largest city in the U.S. in 1986, still had in that year a majority of non-Hispanic whites in its population, throughout the 1980s it experienced the kind of accelerated demographic change that was apparent in Southern California. In 1987, the *Houston Post* reported that from 80,000 to 120,000 El Salvadorans alone were living in the city, which then had a total of possibly as many as 500,000 Hispanics, more than in all of San Antonio.[26] In 1986, the *Wall Street Journal* reported that, while Hispanics accounted for about one-fifth of Houston's total population, they were represented by one-third of the children in the Houston School District.[27] The demographic wave of the future was underscored by the *Houston Post's* observation that "Hispanics make up 55 percent of the first-grade class in the Houston Independent School District but are only 8 percent of the voters." [28] The same newspaper, reporting on "The Changing Face of Houston," succinctly summarized the great demographic shift in the following caption: "The 1960 census recorded no one from Japan, Korea, India or Vietnam living in Houston. The 1980 census recorded 2,219 Japanese, 2,499 Koreans, 6,610 Indians and 9,481 Vietnamese. The Texas Department of Health predicts that the Harris County Hispanic population will increase 264 percent by the year 1999. The white population will increase 39 percent." [29]

Demographic trends which became apparent in south Texas during the 1980s will be dominant throughout Texas in the twenty-first century. In 1986, the *Dallas Morning News* reported that "Before the turn of the century, white children will become a minority in Texas, according to a report released this week by former Labor Secretary F. Ray Marshall and demographer Leon F. Bouvier. By 1995, white children will make up 48 percent of the state's population under age 15. Thirty years from now, young Hispanics will equal Anglos in numbers . . . . Statewide, 30 percent of the public school student population is Hispanic, according to the Texas Education Agency in Austin." [30]

Another article in the *Dallas Morning News* notes that "because of the illegal immigrant population and differing methods of counting the Hispanic population, demographic estimates for that ethnic group vary widely -- from a conservative 25 percent on up to 50 percent by the end of the century." [31] A projection reported in 1987 estimates that Hispanics will become more than 50 percent of the total population of Texas by the year 2050. [32] Even these rather conservative projections foresee a radical transformation in the population of Texas within what, considered from the historian's perspective, is the relatively brief span of but two generations.

In addition to immigration and natural increase, the Hispanic population in the Southwest is being steadily augmented by the influx of refugees. In one week late in 1988, 1,622 Central Americans applied for political asylum at the Immigration and Naturalization Service's office at Harlingen, Texas, although "Very few of them follow up on their applications once they are in the United States." [33] In 1988, it was estimated, by advocates of the Moakley-DeConcini bill, that there were then 500,000 El Salvadorans and 200,000 Nicaraguans, all economic or political refugees, in the U.S. illegally. [34] By the early months of 1989, the influx of refugees had swollen to the point that *Time* concluded that "The hectic scene in southern Texas reflects the confusion of a U.S. immigration policy that is on the verge of being swamped by a virtual tidal wave of new arrivals." [35]

Sol Sanders, writing in *Orbis* in 1988, raised the possibility that in addition to the refugees from the turmoil in Central America, there might one day be millions of Mexicans fleeing revolutionary upheaval in their own country:

> One has only to recall that during the period of 1910-1924, some one-tenth of the Mexican population migrated to the United States. . . . Should a new breakdown occur in Mexico, millions of Mexicans would cross into the United States to avoid the violence and seek a livelihood. The prelude to such a movement is already under way. Some 1.8 million illegal immigrants were taken into U.S. custody at the southern border in 1986, about a million more than in 1985. Large numbers of Mexicans -- perhaps four times as many as those apprehended -- enter the United States every year.[36]

Contrary to popular belief in areas of the U.S. far removed from its southern border, the Immigration Reform and Control Act of 1986 has only partially limited the influx of illegal immigrants into the U.S. First of all, IRCA itself has enabled great numbers of illegal immigrants to become candidates for U.S. citizenship through its amnesty provisions. As of May 5, 1988, more than two million illegal immigrants had applied for amnesty, of whom 70 percent were from Mexico, 8 percent from El Salvador, and 3 percent from Guatemala.[37] The 1.5 million applicants who received legal status "listed over 2.5 million spouses, children and parents on their application forms, almost 900,000 of whom are already illegally in the U.S."[38] When these amnestied aliens become citizens, there will be no legal limit on the numbers of their relatives who may immigrate or, if already in the U.S., become legal permanent residents.

In November 1987, the *Wall Street Journal* headlined an article on the impact of the IRCA as "Spotty Record: Now a Year Old, Immigration Law Has Cut Illegal Border Crossing But Is No Panacea."[39] A.S. Ross, writing in the *San Francisco Examiner* in May 1988, reported that "recent studies show that the number of undocumented aliens crossing the border has returned to pre-Immigration Reform and Control Act levels." Ross quoted a report by the University of California at San Diego's Center for U.S.-Mexican Studies, which concluded that "There is a growing sense of apathy toward the law as undocumented immigrants see that other 'illegals' continue to get jobs."[40]

A report released by the Center in June 1989 asserted that even two years after its implementation, IRCA was still failing to achieve its purpose. According to an account in the *Los Angeles Times,*

> "The 1986 immigration law has not shut off the flow of new undocumented immigrants from . . . Mexico," said Wayne A. Cornelius, director of the Center for U.S.-Mexican Studies and head of the study. "No viable alternative to migrating to the United States has developed in these communities, so they're continuing to send people." Moreover, Cornelius, one of the leading

U.S. experts on Mexico and immigration, said migrants are increasingly arriving from areas of Mexico relatively new to the migrant stream, such as Mexico City and the southern states of Mexico, Guerrero and Oaxaca. The development is an ominous one for U.S. policy-makers seeking to deter illegal immigration, Cornelius said, as it indicates that new migrant networks are being created at a time when authorities would like to seal off arrivals from traditional migrant areas.[41]

In December, 1991, *The New York Times* reported that "New figures released last month by the Immigration and Naturalization Service show that for the fiscal year that ended Sept. 30, apprehensions at the Mexican border rose slightly to 1,077,511 from 1,049,680 in 1990. Both years were up considerably from the 854,128 arrests recorded in 1989, the last of three years that registered a decline."[42]

Whatever the total number of illegal entrants may be -- and those who are not apprehended are at least as numerous as those who are -- once they have eluded the Border Patrol, their detection, apprehension, and deportation becomes uncertain, difficult, and always costly. Moreover, even those who are proved to be illegal entrants may not always be easily deported. According to court decisions, any person born within the territorial limits of the United States is a citizen thereof. Many illegal entrants are the parents of U.S. citizens who were born following their parents' entry into the U.S., paradoxical as that may sound. They can be deported, but not their children. Obviously, however, legal action leading to their deportation will usually not be undertaken in such cases.

There are two significant economic factors which are commonly cited to account for this mass migration into the Southwest. First, it is widely assumed that immigrants are almost exclusively employed in "secondary jobs," ill-paid, seasonal labor that is shunned by natives of the U.S. Secondly, the great differential between average incomes in the U.S. and Mexico is thought to account for most of the impetus behind immigration.

While both of these factors are obviously important, they may not be as salient as they at first seem to be. The first hypothesis correctly assumes a dual labor market in industrialized nations, a market of well-paid positions alongside a market of ill-paid work in the service economy, but there is evidence that not even illegal immigrants are limited to the secondary economy. Michael J. Piore, a leading economist in migration studies, writing in May, 1986 on "The Shifting Grounds for Immigration" notes that many immigrants, after a period of settlement, escape the secondary labor market. The theory of income differentials as the impetus behind the new migration he finds to be even more unsatisfactory because massive immigration historically first came to the U.S. from European nations closest to the U.S. in income levels, then began to emerge from lands having ever lower economic levels compared with that of the U.S. According to the income-differential hypothesis, the first sourceof mass immigration into the U.S. should have been Mexico, not Europe.[43]

A population explosion, more than any other factor, accounts for the impetus behind the new mass migration to the U.S. The population factor has been well summarized, as follows, in Leon Bouvier and David Simcox's *Many Hands, Few Jobs: Population, Unemployment and Emigration in Mexico and the Caribbean:*

> In 1980, the population of the countries of the Caribbean Basin -- Mexico, Central America, the island states, and the littoral nations of Colombia, Venezuela and Guyana -- totalled 166 million. Just 30 years before less than 70 million lived in the region. In those three decades, the population more than doubled, adding more than 96 million. Between 1980 and 2010 -- another 30-year period -- the population will double again, to about 320 million. About 154 million more inhabitants will be added in three decades even though fertility rates should fall considerably. By the year 2025, the Caribbean region's population of 366 million will dwarf the 295 million foreseen for the U.S. Thus, the vigorous growth we see now is little more than the tip of a demographic iceberg.[44]

The skewed age structure of this growing population means that the growth in numbers of young people needing employment will be even more rapid than the overall population growth. According to Bouvier and Simcox, Mexico's labor force, during the last three decades of the century, will increase by 180 percent, its population by a "mere" 113 percent.[45] While Mexico is obliged to produce new work for its people at a rate two-and-one-half times greater than that of the U.S., the nation suffers from massive unemployment and underemployment. Bouvier and Simcox report that the "Noted Mexican economist Victor Urquidi stated in March 1986 that 3.5 million of what he estimated as Mexico's 24-million labor force lacked work. The Mexican magazine *Proceso* reported similar figures in June 1986, . . . totaling 48 percent of the labor force unemployed or underemployed."[46]

Sol Sanders, writing in *Strategic Review* in 1986, sees in Mexico's population explosion the prime mover for both its internal political instability and its continuing export of millions of economically motivated refugees.[47] The Kissinger Commission, appointed in 1984 to study Central America, concluded, in the following terms, that an explosive growth in population is also the primary cause of that area's economic and political problems:

> Unemployment and underemployment are spreading -- overriding social and economic problems in all five countries. The high rate of population growth

magnifies these problems. Job opportunities are vanishing, even as a quarter of a million young people are entering Central America's job market each year. In a region where half the population is below the age of 20, the combination of youth and massive unemployment is a problem of awesome -- and explosive dimensions.[48]

A *Los Angeles Times* poll taken in August 1989 of 1,835 Mexicans revealed that "the country has become so impoverished that half of all Mexican children may suffer from hunger. Asked if their friends' and neighbors' children have enough to eat, 53% of the respondents said 'no' and, among the poor, 69% said the children are sometimes hungry."[49] Extrapolations from poll results led to the conclusion that "more than 4.7 million Mexican citizens believe they are very likely to move north in the next year."[50] The same article noted that "Bustamante [Jorge Bustamante, a Mexican immigration expert and president of Tijuana's Colegio de la Frontera] charges that the Immigration and Naturalization Service tinkered with its figures by stepping up patrols before the immigration legislation was passed by Congress and reducing enforcement since the law went into effect. 'They manipulate the number of hours they dedicate to apprehensions. There is no significant difference between the numbers [of illegal immigrants] last year and this year,' Bustamante said."[51]

By the 1990s, it had become clear that the factors behind the influx of immigrants, whether legal or illegal, were unlikely to change in any foreseeable future. The human flood would continue as long as it was tolerated by the American citizenry.

# II

# *The Limits of Assimilation*

D ue to cultural lag, popular concepts of societal processes often reflect not present realities, but conditions existing during prior decades. Such is the case with the popular concept of assimilation, which is still usually considered to be simply an inevitable process in which ethnic separatism succumbs before the all-resolving centripetal force of a common national culture. This model of assimilation, in which all divergent ethnic groups come to be centered about and then ultimately disappear within a kind of national core culture, is, however, only a superficial description of American reality in the latter years of the twentieth century.

Milton M. Gordon, in his *Assimilation in American Life: The Role of Race, Religion, and National Origins,* has defined three major stages of development of the concept of assimilation. Each has seen the recognition of a new reality regarding assimilation which has more or less violated an older ideal. The ideal of "Anglo-conformity," which "demanded the complete renunciation of the immigrant's ancestral culture in favor of the behavior and values of the Anglo-Saxon core group" prevailed almost until the end of the nineteenth century.[52] It was superseded in the following two decades by the "melting pot" ideal, which heralded "a biological merger of the Anglo-Saxon peoples with other immigrant groups and a blending of their respective cultures into a new indigenous American type."[53] During the 1920s, the ideal of "cultural pluralism" came into vogue, postulating "the preservation of the communal life and significant portions of the culture of the immigrant groups within the context of American citizenship and political and economic integration into American society."[54]

Gordon's "Models of Pluralism: The New American Dilemma," published in 1981, reports evidence, even then apparent, that official public policy had begun to support a new variant of cultural pluralism, one which militates against the earlier ideal of political and economic integration.[55] The new American dilemma, as ominous as the one once addressed by Gunnar Myrdal, is the nation's drift away from its tradition of "liberal pluralism," in which "government gives no formal recognition to categories of people based on race or ethnicity," and towards a new, "corporate pluralism," which "envisages a nation where its racial and ethnic entities are formally recognized as such -- are given formal standing as groups in the national polity -- and where patterns of political power and economic reward are based on a distributive formula which postulates group rights and which defines group membership as an important factor in the outcome for individuals."[56]

Gordon believes that corporate pluralism is a growing reality, not simply a possible alternative, because "recently introduced measures such as government-mandated affirmative action procedures in employment, education, and stipulated public programs, and court-ordered busing of school children across neighborhood district lines to effect racial integration, constitute steps toward the corporate pluralist idea."[57] Since corporate pluralism replaces "individual meritocracy" with "group rewards," it strongly discourages assimilation in the conventional sense because "if a significant portion of one's rational interests are likely to be satisfied by emphasis on one's ethnicity, then one might as well stay within ethnic boundaries and at the same time enjoy the social comforts of being 'among people of one's own kind,' . . . . Moving across ethnic boundaries to engage in significant inter-ethnic social relationships is likely to lead to social marginality in a society where ethnicity and ethnic identity are such salient features. Thus the logic of corporate pluralism is to emphasize structural separation."[58]

While the federal government promotes corporate pluralism by making it the basis for distributing entitlements of all varieties -- admissions to higher education, scholarships, research grants, employment, business contracts, political appointments, etc. -- certain factors in the market economy also encourage the ethnic separatism that undergirds corporate pluralism. There is evidence that family-owned enterprises within their ethnic enclaves may offer greater economic rewards to immigrants than does employment in the mainstream economy. Moreover, as ethnic enclaves grow in population and area, they can sustain even the largest of corporate enterprises, wholly owned and operated by members of that ethnic community, and retaining all profits within the community.[59]

In 1982, Alejandro Portes, a leading scholar in migration studies, concluded from his study of over 1,400 Cubans and Mexicans in the U.S. that "the conventional strategy of resettlement -- dispersal of the immigrant population -- is not necessarily the best route for successful adaptation . . . . Contrary to the view of immigrant enterprise as exploitative of recent immigrants, the Cubans who stayed in Miami, in the enclave, seemed to do somewhat better economically'' than the Mexicans who were dispersed across the country; "Immigrant enclaves tend to promote self-employment. Their absence tends to keep immigrants in wage labor. Self-employed immigrants and others working within an ethnic enclave seem to do better than those in wage labor on the outside.''[60] While one-third of the Mexicans had no knowledge of English after six years of residence in the U.S., fully 45 percent of the Cubans had no such knowledge after the same period; living in the Miami area, which had Spanish-language media, the Cubans had less need to learn English than did the more widely scattered Mexicans, whose greater degree of cultural assimilation did not yield for them the benefit of upward economic mobility enjoyed by the Cubans. Lawrence H. Fuchs, executive director of the Select Commission on Immigration and Refugee Policy, endorsed Portes's conclusions, saying that "You can't force people to stay apart from their friends and relatives and countrymen.''[61] In corroboration of this, an extensive survey published in 1988 by James P. Allen and Eugene J. Turner, geographers at California State University, Northridge, concluded that 90 percent of immigrants choose to live in a metropolitan area.[62]

The concentration of Mexican immigrants was noted, as follows, in a RAND Corporation report published in mid-1991 in *Science:*

Today more than half of the Mexican-origin population is residing in the western United States (primarily in California), and this regional concentration is increasing. The relative concentration of the Mexican-born population in this region increased from 52 percent in 1960 to 64 percent in 1980. No other foreign-origin population is nearly as concentrated in one region . . . . this population is further highly concentrated within selected county and city jurisdictions. Within the western region, in 1980, 87 percent of the Mexican-born population and nearly 80 percent of the Mexican-origin population lived in metropolitan areas, including Los Angeles, San Diego, Fresno, San Jose, San Antonio, Houston, and Phoenix. At current relative rates of growth, it will soon constitute a majority population in an increasing number of jurisdictions, most particularly in California.[63]

Since the massive influx of Mexican and Central American immigrants into the Southwest followed that of the Cubans into Miami by almost two decades, the former groups are rather delayed in establishing their own "enclave economy." However, in a couple of decades, at the most, the new Hispanic immigrants in the Southwest should be able to replicate the achievements of the Cubans (and other Hispanics) in the Miami area. By then, most cities in the Southwest, as well as wide expanses of non-urban territory, will have attained the degree of ethnic and socio-economic division that had become glaringly apparent in the Miami area at the close of the 1980s.

Surveying Miami early in 1989, two reporters for the *Miami Herald* found a tripartite division in virtually all aspects of the area's economic and cultural life. They epitomized this division in the following terms:

> In business, the Greater Miami Chamber of Commerce, despite its name, shares the county stage with the Latin Chamber of Commerce and the mostly black Miami-Dade Chamber of Commerce. In law, attorneys network at the Dade County Bar Association, the Cuban-American Bar Association and the Black Lawyers Association. Women climb the executive ladder through the National Association of Women Business Owners, the Coalition of Hispanic American Women and the predominantly black Business and Professional Women's Club. At Alcoholics Anonymous, Latins can sober up with Latins, blacks with blacks, Anglos with Anglos. In Opa-Locka, veterans share war stories at two posts on the same street, one black and one white. Poor cancer patients find a place of last resort at La Liga Contra el Cancer, once a branch of the American Cancer Society transplanted from Cuba but today an independent outfit whose patients are overwhelmingly Hispanic. They cure the same diseases, drive the same tractors, teach from the same books -- but Dade's dentists, doctors, educators, journalists, building contractors, accountants, police officers, even debutantes and bowlers seek strength in their own kind.[64]

The example of Miami underscores the error in equating the successful economic settlement of aliens in a nation with their assimilation of the culture of that nation. Michael J. Piore, whose *Birds of Passage: Migrant Labor and Industrial Societies* is a definitive study of the economic factors governing mass migration from the Third World to the industrialized nations, defines as follows the relationship and distinction between settlement and assimilation:

> The transition envisaged by the melting pot is a process of *assimilation* in which the migrant, *through contact with the industrial culture,* absorbs its attitudes and values. The transition involved in settlement is an autonomous process that occurs within the immigrant community independently of whatever contacts that community has with the larger cultural environment in which it is situated. To the extent that settlement results in a set of values coincident with those of the native population, it is because in the settlement process the subjective relationship of the migrant worker to his economic environment comes to resemble that of the native population, not because the former has *borrowed* the values of the latter.[65]

The most significant fact concerning the geographic location of Hispanic immigrants in the U.S. is, however, not their concentration in urban neighborhoods, but rather their closeness to their countries of origin. Thousands of miles separated earlier immigrants from their homelands in Europe, but many Mexican American immigrants live only the proverbial stone's throw away from their nation of birth. Even Mexican Americans born in the U.S. can realistically regard Mexico as their cultural homeland because millions of them live close enough to the border to allow trips there and back of short duration. This closeness of millions of an ethnic group to their ancestral or native homeland is a unique situation in the immigration history of the U.S. On the basis of geography alone, then, it is patently absurd to claim that Hispanic immigration must follow the pattern of past immigration from Europe.

This geographic closeness to the nation of their ancestors may account more than any other factor for the failure of assimilation reported by James W. Lemare in 1982 in *International Migration Review*. Lemare studied 700 Mexican American children, aged nine through fourteen years, living in El Paso, Texas, all of them children of first through fifth generation immigrants. He found that "Overall, Mexican-American children, regardless of generation, show only limited commitment to the American political community. To be sure, each generation professes a preference for living in the United States, but only the mixed and second generation consider this to be the best country. None of the five cohorts prefers the label 'American' over identification tags more reflective of their national origin. Lastly, no generation exhibits a strong sense of trust in others.'"[66]

A study of Hispanic adults undertaken in 1984 by the polling firm of Yankelovich, Skelly & White included Hispanics throughout the U.S. This sample included Puerto Ricans in New York City and Cubans in Miami who are either geographically or politically more distant from their nations of origin than are Mexicans and Central Americans. Slightly more subjects polled in 1984 considered themselves "Hispanic first, American second" (50 percent) than did so in 1981 (46 percent). In 1984, 84 percent of those polled agreed that it is important for them to preserve the Spanish language, compared with 81 percent so agreeing in 1981. In 1984, 74 percent of those polled stated that bilingualism was their goal in language usage, while 20 percent chose fluency in Spanish, and 6 percent fluency in English.[67]

A similar study conducted in 1989 by Strategy Research Corporation, a Miami-based market research firm, was based on 4,500 random door-to-door interviews conducted with Hispanics in all of the 29 largest Hispanic markets in the U.S. Eight out of 10 interviewees described themselves as Hispanic first and American second. According to the *San Diego Tribune's* report of the study, "Nearly 40 percent of Hispanics in the United States have failed to assimilate into the culture and may spend their lives immersed in communities where Spanish is the only language needed to survive, . . . The study concluded this segment will find it can exist very well without learning English, remaining immersed in Spanish-language media, products, civic organizations and value systems.'"[68]

The results of the Strategy Research Corporation's study were confirmed in

1991, when David Hayes-Bautista, head of the Chicano Studies Research Center at the University of California at Los Angeles, published his three-year study of cultural attitudes among 1,000 Hispanics in the U.S. Some significant conclusions from this research were published in *The New York Times* as follows: "'We could come back in 100 years and the Latinos will not have assimilated in the classic sense,' Dr. Hayes-Bautista said. 'I'm pretty sure they will still have a sense of being Latinos.' . . . In Dr. Hayes-Bautista's study, many respondents said that Hispanic history should be taught in schools and that children should maintain their family's Hispanic culture. Most tellingly, these attitudes, along with a working knowledge of Spanish, were maintained to a significant degree through the third generation and beyond.'"[69]

Leo Estrada, a demographer at the University of California at Los Angeles who specializes in Hispanic immigration, said of the findings in the study, again according to the *Times:* "'He actually finds that the sequence that would be expected, from immigrant to second generation and on to becoming homogeneous, gets arrested.' . . . Speaking of people who travel frequently to Mexico from their homes in the American Southwest for a birthday party or a weekend, Dr. Estrada said: 'They never thought of themselves as having left totally. I think one of the most remarkable things I see is the number of people to whom the border has become artificial.'"[70]

Hispanic immigrants are encouraged to retain fluency in their native language by the burgeoning Spanish-language broadcasting industry. More and more Spanish-language radio and television stations are beginning broadcasting in response to a growing Hispanic audience and market. The July 25, 1988, issue of *Television/Radio Age* reported that "While the [Bozell, Jacobs, Kenyon & Eckhardt] agency notes there are 10 Spanish TV stations in the U.S. and 54 radio stations, the number of Spanish-language stations is known to be considerably higher than this. Reps serving Hispanic radio stations put the number at 190 full-time stations."[71] The same issue notes that the Lempert marketing analysis firm "reports growth in advertising expenditures to the Hispanic market will be about 25% a year for the next five years, compared with overall ad spending increases of about 8% annually."[72] In a survey of "Bright Prospects for Speaking Spanish," the September 26, 1988, issue of *Broadcasting* quotes Gene Bryan of Katz Hispanic Radio as predicting that "We're at the tip of the iceberg of what Spanish radio will be in the 21st century."[73]

While the private sector, acting from economic motives, sustains non-English-speaking ethnic enclaves, the federal government has moved public policy from the monolingualism which had remained unchallenged in the U.S. since the beginning of the twentieth century, to bilingualism, and even a kind of "affirmative ethnicity."[74] In 1968, Title VII, which mandated the now-growing bilingual education program, was added to the Elementary and

Secondary Education Act of 1962.[75] In 1975, the Voting Rights Act of 1965 was amended to require bilingual elections in areas where a linguistic minority group comprises five percent or more of the population.[76]

Linda Chavez, briefly president of U.S. English, is almost a lone exception among Hispanic American leaders in warning that acceptance of bilingualism means that ''the United States could be faced in the 21st century with the same kind of language divisions that plague our northern neighbor today.''[77] Most prominent Hispanic Americans agree with the sentiments expressed in former Miami mayor Maurice Ferre's bold prediction in 1982 that ''within 10 years there will not be a word of English spoken -- English is not Miami's official language -- one day residents will learn Spanish or leave.''[78] The proliferation of advertisements in the Miami area stipulating that applicants for employment must be bilingual or Spanish-speaking has given a grim reality to Ferre's forecast.[79]

Some Hispanic spokesmen almost seem to herald a kind of cultural *reconquista* which is to begin in the public school classroom. Typical of this cultural militancy is the following observation by Robert Cordova, a professor of Spanish writing in the *Houston Chronicle:* ''To prepare American youth for the America and world of the not-too-distant future, the present monolingual, monocultural Anglocentric public education system must be replaced by a multilingual, multicultural, pluralistic one . . . . The Hispanic population is becoming larger and Hispanic culture is becoming stronger . . . . American society and ideas of old no longer exist.''[80]

Ricardo Chavira, who reports on the U.S. State Department for *Time* magazine, expresses the same sentiments in the following, rather more pungent terms: ''Imagine the ludicrousness of an elementary school teacher telling a room full of Chicanos that George Washington and company were our Founding Fathers. Obviously, those guys in matching white wigs were no fathers of mine.''[81]

The kind of ''affirmative ethnicity'' defended by Ferre, Cordova, Chavira and others will prevail over the traditional ideal of assimilation when those who are to be assimilated begin to outnumber, in ever-greater areas, those who are to bring about the assimilation. Only a subconscious ethnocentrism can account for the belief that an ethnic minority, which the ''Anglos'' will eventually be in most areas of the Southwest, may in a liberal democracy determine the language, culture and values of an ethnic majority. Such attempts have invariably been undertaken by means of coercive state power and justified by elitist or racist ideologies which are now consciously repudiated by the nation's governing stratum.

Concomitant with this shift of public policy away from ''Anglo-conformity'' as a strategy of assimilation is a growing rejection within the nation's educational system of what is denounced as ''Eurocentrism,'' an allegedly

European bias in the teaching of literature, history, and other subjects. The argument against this supposed "Eurocentrism" has been trenchantly stated, in the following words, by Molefi Asante, chairman of African American studies at Temple University: "We are not living in a Western country. The American project is not yet completed. It is only in the eyes of the Eurocentrists who see it as a Western project, which means to hell with the rest of the people who have yet to create the project." Asante would supplement the "Eurocentric" view with an "Afrocentric and Latinocentric" view of the world.[82] The triumph of this educational philosophy within the nation's public school systems would, obviously, lead to a reinforcement of corporate pluralism, the precise opposite of assimilation in the commonly received sense of the word.

By 1989, many responsible observers were beginning to admit openly that the Los Angeles area could no longer be understood in terms of older models of assimilation. Frederick Rose reported that year in the *Wall Street Journal* that

> Seers suggest that Los Angeles will not be an assimilationist "melting pot" but will remain a mix of cultures and economies that are discrete and retain strong ties to other countries. LA 2000, a committee appointed by Mayor Tom Bradley to look at the city's future, recently concluded that Los Angeles in the next century will be "not just a bigger world center, but a kind of international city of cities . . . ." . . . ."Los Angeles," predicts Richard Weinstein, the dean of architecture and urban studies at the University of California at Los Angeles, "will be the first American metropolis of the Third World." . . . That pressures might someday explode in violence of the sort once seen in Watts worries people like Lewis H. Butler, the president of California Tomorrow, a think tank specializing in immigration and ethnicity. "Los Angeles could be so fragmented that it could be a very unpleasant place to live," he says.[83]

In mid-1991, Benjamin Mark Cole reported in the *Los Angeles Business Journal* that the city was beginning to experience the polarization of classes that typifies a Third World city: "Metropolis Los Angeles, a middle-class stronghold through the 1960s -- a refuge for Depression-era Okies and Arkies, and *lebensraum* for winter-bound Iowans and New Yorkers -- now is becoming a land of wealth and poverty, a type of modern Dickensian hell. Increasingly, it is becoming an Americanized version of a Third World nation's capital city, growing dependent on cheap labor as its middle class vanishes and wealth eyes poverty across walled barriers."[84]

As examples of this economic polarization, Cole cites the juxtaposition of Beverly Hills and Bel Air against Cudahy and Bell Gardens, communities having "per capita incomes below that of East St. Louis, the Midwest town

routinely portrayed in national media as the country's most wretched munici-
pality.'' Cole quotes Goetz Wolff, an industrial economist, as saying that
''We are creating a two-tiered society of haves and have-nots. And realistically, it is only going to get worse.''[85] Cole also cites numerous statistics to
substantiate this assessment, reporting changes in income distribution that
indicate a slow disappearance of the middle class: ''By one estimate, the
fraction of upper-income households in Los Angeles, defined as those with
incomes exceeding $50,000, tripled to 27 percent in the 1980s, while the
fraction of families with incomes below $15,000 rose to 40 percent from 30
percent. The middle class shrank to 32 percent from 61 percent, by these
definitions.''[86]

Cole attributes this development to ''Two decades of heavy immigration,
feeble labor law enforcement and a loss of heavy manufacturing jobs.''[87] The
resulting ''economic ghetto'' of often-exploited legal and illegal immigrants
can only have the effect of halting any process of assimilation in the conventional sense of the term.

It had also become apparent by mid-1991 that ethnic divisions in California
extended to the campus of the University of California at Berkeley, the one
place where one might expect such divisions to be overcome by a sense of
cosmopolitanism. Noting this, Ernest L. Boyer, former U.S. Education Commissioner and president of the Carnegie Foundation for the Advancement of
Teaching, asked, ''If humanism and communal understanding can't happen
on a college campus, how in the world can it happen on city streets?''[88]

Miami, however, rather than humanism, proved to be the archetype for
student associations at Berkeley where, according to an account in *The New
York Times,* ''At lunchtime, Sproul Plaza becomes an international bazaar:
members of the Filipino-American Alliance are there, as are members of the
Vietnamese Students' Association, the Chinese Student Association, the
Asian Student Union and Tonodach; the Japanese American Cultural Club.
Students can join the Asian Business Association, attend a Black Sociology
Student Association meeting or go to the Hispanic Engineering Society dance,
if they belong to the right group.''[89]

Such divisions among students were not remarkable, however, given their
presence even among their mentors, according to an account published two
years earlier in the *San Francisco Examiner:* ''Racial labels are commonly
used among academics in Southern California to refer to the different UC
campuses. Irvine, which will have a 42.2 percent Asian American freshman
class this fall, is called the 'yellow campus'; UCLA, with 9 percent black and
20 percent Hispanic, the 'black and brown' campus; and Santa Barbara, 62
percent white, the 'white' campus.''[90]

Among high school-aged youth, ethnic divisions were increasingly manifested as gangs. In 1989, the Los Angeles county Human Relations Commis-

sion reported that "hate crimes" had been committed at 37 percent of the county's 950 public schools. In mid-1991, the *Los Angeles Times* reported that "black and Latino students have clashed in Inglewood, while Latino, Vietnamese and Chinese students have fought in the San Gabriel Valley."[91] In Long Beach, 18 months of gang warfare between Hispanic and Cambodian gangs resulted in "more than 55 drive-by shootings, . . . including 10 people shot to death . . . . Fears of violence have nearly paralyzed the city's Cambodian population of about 45,000 . . . . Shops and restaurants are losing business and a few residents are moving away. Cambodian New Year's celebrations last month, which in the past have attracted visitors from around the country, were all but canceled."[92]

Hitherto unknown intergroup tensions and violence seemed to be becoming the rule, rather than the exception. Building up to an unprecedented vehemence, they exploded into the riots that took place in south central Los Angeles during May 1992. Jack Miles, book editor for the *Los Angeles Times,* contributed a lengthy analysis of the ethnic conflicts involved to the October 1992 issue of the *Atlantic Monthly*. Pointedly entitled "Blacks vs. Browns," Miles's article argues that uncontrolled Hispanic immigration has been even more detrimental than Asian business acumen to the economic interests of African Americans. He believes that this explains why the rioters' fury so frequently found a target in businesses owned by Asians and Hispanics.[93]

The Los Angeles riots of 1992, because they involved mutual antagonisms among three distinct ethnic blocs, marked the advent of a new, more complex, and more troubling phase in the history of inter-group conflict in America. It is perhaps not unjustified to draw a parallel between the destruction wrought upon the Asian merchants of Los Angeles and that suffered in the same year by the Moslems of Bosnia in the name of "ethnic cleansing." When three different groups are polarized in as many different directions, and this polarization erupts into sporadic episodes of violence, then there can be no question of assimilation. Merely keeping the peace must become the focus of all energies.

Throughout the 1980s, the reaction of "Anglos" to this ongoing failure of assimilation was largely limited to attempts to promote a superficial "Anglo-conformity" by demanding legislation to establish English as an "official language." These efforts usually took the form of state legislative acts or referenda aimed to establish English as the state's official language. By the end of 1988, seventeen states had enacted legislation or passed referenda recognizing English as the state's official language.[94]

Some of the most embittered political battles emerging from the language question have taken place in urban areas, beginning with Miami in 1980.[95] In California, the mayor of Monterey Park, which had by the mid-1980s a plurality of speakers of Chinese, received much publicity for his statements deploring the proliferation of Chinese language business signs.[96] Nearby cities in California have passed legislation stipulating how much English must appear on business signs (in Temple City, 100% in English downtown, 50% in outlying areas; in Arcadia, 70%; in Pomona and Rosemead, 50%).[97]

By 1990, Monterey Park had a new mayor, a Chinese-American; the Chinese-American population had grown to comprise 60 percent of the total; and Chinese language business signs were no longer subject to legal challenge. Civic groups sought to mediate differences between ethnic groups in a multitude of ways; "for example, a city-sponsored 'Harmony Week' of essay contests on how to live in a multiracial community."[98] However, the relative calm may have been largely due to the subsidence of nativist opposition. The mayor's description of parallel organizations was reminiscent of the ethnic polarization of Miami: "We have a Kiwanis Club and an Asian Kiwanis Club, a Lion's Club and an Asian Lion's Club, a Monterey Park Democratic Club and a Monterey Park Asian Democratic Club."[99]

Different nationalities of Asians have concentrated themselves in different cities of California, thus preserving linguistic "islands." *The Economist* thus described some of these in 1990:

> Economic expansion may have transformed the physical face of California, but by far the greatest social and economic changes in the past ten years have been wrought by foreign immigration. The signs are everywhere. The port city of Long Beach, once known as 'Iowa by the sea', is now home to 40,000 Cambodians. Daly City outside San Francisco, once a mostly white, blue-collar town, is now called 'Little Manila' because of its large Filipino population. Fresno, a farming town in the Central Valley, has become home to 30,000 Hmong, a Laotian hill tribe. A stretch of shops and malls between Garden Grove and Westminster in Orange County conjures up a vision of what Saigon might look like, if it were lucky enough to enjoy American-style affluence. Some 80,000 Vietnamese refugees live in the area and thousands more visit it at weekends to shop and socialise.[100]

Much publicity was given during the 1980s to a proposal to have English made the official language of the U.S. by an amendment to the U.S. Constitution. A formidable political stumbling-block in the way of the enactment of such an "English only" amendment, one which would also remain to impede its enforcement, is the legal status of Spanish in one state, New Mexico, and in a potential state, Puerto Rico.

When a bill to make English the official language of the state of New Mexico was introduced in that state's legislature, it was soundly defeated after only forty minutes of debate. Opposition was not limited to Hispanic legislators, but arose largely because its passage would have overruled the provision of New Mexico's constitution which requires training of teachers in both

English and Spanish and publication of legislative documents in Spanish.[101]

On February 6, 1990, Judge Paul G. Rosenblatt of the 5th U.S. District Court, ruled unconstitutional an Arizona law making English the language "of all government functions and actions" in the state. The law, an amendment to Arizona's constitution, violated the First Amendment of the U.S. Constitution, Judge Rosenblatt ruled, because it forbade all public officials and employees to use any language other than English in communicating with their constituents.[102]

In his first address to the U.S. Congress, President George Bush asked the members of that body to authorize Puerto Ricans, almost all of whom are Spanish-speaking, to vote on whether their island should become a state, an independent nation, or remain a self-governing possession of the U.S. In a memorandum of November 30, 1992, President Bush directed "all Federal departments, agencies, and officials, to the extent consistent with the Constitution and the laws of the United States, henceforward to treat Puerto Rico administratively as if it were a state."[103] If, as it seems probable, Puerto Rico becomes a state, it will be even more difficult to argue that Spanish cannot be the official language of a state.

While he was still mayor of Miami, Maurice Ferre, in the following words, welcomed statehood for Puerto Rico for precisely that reason:

> Now here come those Puerto Ricans. And they're saying, "Wait a minute. Not only can you not discriminate against me because I'm Catholic. Because I happen to have some black blood in me. And because I happen to be a youngster or a female. You can't discriminate against me because I happen to speak a different language." *That's* the line. *Permanently* speaking a different language. And that's when America really becomes America . . . . Let's get the definition. Not transitional Spanish. We're talking about Spanish as a main form of communication. As an official language. Not on the way to English. What I'm saying is that what color is to blacks, language is to Hispanics. And that's something that has to be very clearly understood.[104]

Throughout the history of the United States, the states have been allowed to legislate the status of language or languages in their governments and school systems. However, even when many states enacted legislation to suppress the use of a language, German, no corresponding movement arose on the federal level to amend the Constitution. James C. Stalker, writing in *English Journal,* official organ of the National Council of Teachers of English, summarized in the following the history of permissiveness in this regard: "The Louisiana constitution allowed the publication of laws in French, and they were so published until about seventy years ago. California (1849) and Texas allowed the publication of laws in Spanish, and New Mexico still maintained Spanish and English as official languages of the state until 1941. In 1842 Texas required the publication of its laws in German as well as Spanish and English and added Norwegian in 1858."[105] Languages used in public schools in Hawaii and Minnesota were long subject to local option.[106]

There is also evidence that the campaign to establish English is encountering a counter-movement of "affirmative ethnicity." A hint of this is evident in the recommendation in 1988 of the Texas state legislature's Select Committee on Education that Spanish be made a required subject in the public schools, beginning with the elementary schools.[107] In 1989, elementary school students in at least one area in Southern California were required to learn Spanish even if they were "Anglos" having English as their mother tongue. According to an account in the *Los Angeles Times,* "At Edison Elementary School in a Latino section of Santa Monica, kindergarten and first-grade pupils are taught in Spanish except for one oral English class, regardless of whether students' parents speak English or Spanish. English-language classes are gradually added, working up to a 50-50 language mix in sixth grade. 'The Edison School project assumes that both Hispanics and Anglos will emerge competent in both languages,' said Russell N. Campbell, a UCLA linguistics professor."[108]

Advocates of bilingual education won a significant victory early in 1989 when William J. Bennett was replaced as head of the U.S. Department of Education by Lauro F. Cavazos, who selected Rita Esquivel to head the department's bilingual education program.[109] While Bennett opposed extension of bilingual education programs, believing that all students should be placed in classrooms where English is the sole language of instruction, Esquivel, former assistant superintendent of California's Santa Monica-Malibu Unified School District, favored use of the child's native language as a "bridge" to instruction in English. Cavazos' belief that "At the same time that we are teaching our children English, we must do all we can to help them to maintain their native language and culture" was characterized by Shelly Spiegel-Coleman, president of the California Association of Bilingual Education, as a change from Bennett's views that was "very radical, like night and day."[110]

Those who would attempt to make English the official language of the U.S. have taken for a model the forced linguistic assimilation of German-speaking immigrants. This model is flawed, however, in its application to Spanish-speaking immigrants. While speakers of German could not take their children on a weekend excursion to visit the grandparents in the old country, speakers of Spanish are often only a short automobile trip away from their linguistic homeland. In addition, German immigrants ceased to enter the U.S. in significant numbers after 1914. Spanish-speaking immigrants and visitors will continue to enter the U.S. in significant numbers for the forseeable future.

Even if all of the new immigrants, in violation of their Constitutional rights, could somehow be forced to abandon use of their native tongues and to use only English, their assimilation would still be far from being accomplished. After passing through an acculturation process involving language, customs, styles of work and consumption, the new immigrants will largely remain separate and distinct. This is because the overwhelming majority of them belong to visible minorities, minorities already long present in American society which have not been assimilated precisely because of their visibility.

Gordon W. Allport, in his classic study, *The Nature of Prejudice,* stresses the salience of visibility in the genesis of prejudice and borrows from the physical anthropologist Sir Arthur Keith the following scheme for classifying grades of visibility:

Pandiacritic = every individual recognizable

Macrodiacritic = 80 percent or more recogniable

Mesodiacritic = 30-80 percent recognizable

Microdiacritic = less than 30 percent recognizable.

According to Allport's interpretation of this scheme, most of America's new immigrants (i.e., non-white Hispanics, Asians, black Africans and Haitians) are macrodiacritic. Europeans, however, upon losing their foreign accents are mostly microdiacritic, mesodiacritic at most. According to research reported by Allport, Jews, at 55 percent recognizable, are mesodiacritic.[111]

History demonstrates that a macrodiacritic minority, even one consisting of speakers of English, can be fully accepted within the public sphere of American society (e.g., employment, education, public accommodations, civic affairs) only after a long struggle. Such a minority remains largely unassimilated in the private sector of society; i.e., all areas of life (e.g., private associations, churches, clubs, cliques, friends, family) where individual, albeit prejudiced, freedom of choice may still prevail. A superficial behavioral assimilation should not be equated with a fundamental structural assimilation. Cultural assimilation can be coeval with structural pluralism. Such has been the situation in American society from its earliest beginnings.

The new immigration has brought into the United States great numbers of people who do not speak English and who belong to macrodiacritic minority groups. They, moreover, are concentrated geographically in particular regions and urban areas. The latter fact is especially salient because in many areas those who are to be assimilated are beginning to outnumber those to whom they are to be assimilated. It would not be remarkable, therefore, if a continued influx of immigrants were to bring about, in some areas, a process of what might be called ''reverse assimilation.''

Reverse assimilation seems at first thought to be preposterous only because the conventional concept of assimilation is overly simplistic. It can and does occur when a sufficiently large number of immigrants having one origin move into a limited geographical area. It has occurred in American history in at least one instance involving a microdiacritic, foreign-speaking minority, Norwegians in Wisconsin. According to Frank C. Nelson, writing in 1981 in the *Journal of Ethnic Studies,*

"Resignation to assimilation" was followed by a period of "renewed ethnicity," and lasted from 1870 to 1900 . . . . With large numbers of Norwegians coming to America there emerged a significant shift in attitude from the "resignation to assimilation." There developed a new attitude that Norwegians ought "not to be too quick to mimic everything American before we have tested whether it is better than our own." The churches of the Norwegian immigrants played a significant role in promoting this new spirit. As the Lutheran church and other church bodies became stronger as a result of the influx of new members, the congregations began to strongly oppose assimilation and accommodation to American society . . . . A strategy of the Norwegian immigrant clergy was to keep the immigrants from learning English and prevent the erosion of their membership by the aggressive American churches. The period between 1870 and 1900 has been called "the Norwegian period." At this time the Norwegian language had been established as the language of the family, church, and neighborhood . . . . Signs of Norwegian culture were increasingly evident in Norwegian settlements. The Norwegian writer Kristofer Janson lectured to the Norwegian immigrant settlements in 1879-80. When he visited Scandinavia, Wisconsin, he was impressed by Scandinavia's close resemblance to a small community in Norway: "On the streets, in stores, one heard only Norwegian . . . ." The Lutheran church of 1900 was more ethnic than it had been a half century earlier. It had become so as a result of the large numbers of new immigrants and the emergence of an ethnicity long repressed. This new spirit of ethnic awareness was expressed in an editorial in a Norwegian language newspaper: ". . . . Until recently it was a common belief that the Norwegian language would inside a few years be 'dead as a doornail.' We could already hear the funeral bells peal . . . but now, instead of a funeral, we are witnessing the march of triumph." ". . . the Norwegian language had become so popular that it was not only being studied by persons of Norwegian descent but even by Yankees, Irishmen, and Jews." No statistics reveal how many Yankees, Irishmen, and Jews were learning Norwegian for sheer joy alone.[112]

Reverse assimilation came to a halt among Wisconsin's Norwegians because (1) the influx of new immigrants almost ceased after 1900 and (2) the microdiacritic Norwegians could not be easily distinguished, either by others or by themselves, among the mass of other northern Europeans in the state. As of the mid-1990s, of course, neither of these circumstances applied to slow down, much less halt, the reverse assimilation taking place in Miami and Monterey Park and elsewhere.

When reverse assimilation becomes affirmative ethnicity, a conscious movement, it can assume many different forms and adopt as many different strategies. Anthony D. Smith, a British sociologist writing in 1981 in his *The Ethnic Revival,* recognizes six of these and defines them as follows:

> 1. Isolation . . . . the most common strategy for smaller ethnic communities in the past . . . .
> 2. Accommodation. Here the ethnic community aims to adjust to its host society by encouraging its members to participate in the social and political life of the society and its state . . . .
> 3. Communalism . . . . is simply a more dynamic and active form of accommodation . . . . The aim is communal control over communal affairs in those geographical areas where the ethnic community forms a demographic majority.
> 4. Autonomism. There are . . . various forms and degrees of autonomy . . . . Cultural autonomy implies full control by representatives of the ethnic community over every aspect of its cultural life, notably education, the press and mass media, and the courts. Political autonomy or "home rule" extends this to cover every aspect of social, political, and economic life, except for foreign affairs and defense. Ideally, autonomists demand a federal state structure, and this strategy is really only open to communities with a secure regional base.
> 5. Separatism. This is the classic political goal of ethnonational self-determination . . . . In each case, the aim is to secede and form one's own sovereign state, with little or no connection with former rulers.
> 6. Irredentism. Here an ethnic community, whose members are divided and fragmented in separate states, seeks reunification and recovery of the "lost" or "unredeemed" territories occupied by its members. In general, this is only possible where the ethnic community has its membership living in adjoining states or areas.[113]

Obviously, each of these strategies shades into another. They are ranged along a continuum in which the last, irredentism, has its necessary antecedent in the first, isolation. The Cubans in Miami and the Asians in Monterey Park have advanced to the stage of communalism. Neither of these groups, regardless of where they live, has produced adherents of the more advanced strategies. Both groups are, perhaps, too few in number to practice autonomism or separatism, while irredentism is historically meaningless for them. The Mexican Americans of the Southwest, however, great in numbers and possessing a different history, are producing spokesmen for the advanced strategies of autonomism, separatism, and even irredentism.

# III
## The Rise of MexAmerica

A lthough the reluctance of new immigrants to give up their native tongue and the culture and mores of their parents is not unusual, the proximity of the Spanish-speaking ''old country'' to the English-speaking ''new country,'' which is unusual, undergirds that reluctance in many ways and provides a framework for it that extends far beyond the classrooms of the Southwest. During the 1980s, the counter-assimilative effect of that proximity had begun to transform the Southwest into a *de facto* nation which was something other than the southwestern quadrant of the *de jure* nation of the United States of America, yet not simply an extension of old Mexico. In 1981, Joel Garreau devoted a chapter of his book, *The Nine Nations of North America,* to this *de facto* nation, which he called ''MexAmerica.'' By 1988, ''MexAmerica'' had grown to become the topic of an entire book by Lester D. Langley, *MexAmerica: Two Countries, One Future*.

Langley sees MexAmerica as a *de facto* nation which is culturally intermediate between the Anglo America to its north and the Indian America which begins immediately south of Mexico City. This *de facto* nation he optimistically defines as the future product of a fusion of the two old countries. He defines the extent and boundaries of MexAmerica as follows:

> If one considers the concentration of Mexican Americans as geographical indicator, then the northern boundary of Mexico is not the Rio Grande . . . or the barbed wire fence separating Arizona and the Mexican state of Sonora, but a swathlike brushstroke meandering across southern California through central Arizona and New Mexico, then plunging across the arid Texas west toward San Antonio and then on to the Gulf. The southern boundary is more precise -- the populated regions of central Mexico. Southeast of the city of the Incas lies Indian Mexico, another world.[114]

27

While Garreau and Langley stressed the linguistic and cultural factors behind the emergence of MexAmerica, by the close of the 1980s, economic and political factors had become apparent that were fully as significant. Although the linguistic and cultural distinctiveness of the area may be dismissed as something superficial, beneath this superstructure there is a growing economic infrastructure, one which belongs neither to the advanced industrial society of the United States, considered as a nation of the First World, nor to the Third World nation of Indian Mexico. Towards the end of the 1980s, this economic reality had found its political defenders and promoters, most of whom represented interests finding profit in the emergence of this strange new hybrid economy.

Much of the population of MexAmerica is concentrated in urban areas distributed along the U.S.-Mexican border. Several large metropolitan areas in the U.S. (San Diego and Imperial County in California; Tucson, Arizona; Las Cruces, New Mexico; El Paso, Laredo, McAllen, and Brownsville in Texas) had matching *municipios* directly across the border (Tijuana, Mexicali, Nogales, Juarez, Nuevo Laredo, Reynosa, Matamoros). As of 1990, almost eight million people lived in these densely populated areas, 4.8 million in the U.S. and 3 million in Mexico.[115]

Typifying these "twin cities" of MexAmerica is "Los Dos Laredos," where, according to Laredo city manager Peter Vargas, "We're more like Minneapolis and St. Paul than the U.S. and Mexico, because we are the same people."[116] As of 1990, 350,000 people lived in "Los Dos Laredos," 218,000 in Mexico and 132,000 in the U.S., 96 percent of the latter being of Hispanic origin. "You don't even have such a completely Hispanic population in Spain," says Michael Landeck, director of the Institute for International Trade at Laredo State University.[117]

The rise of an atypical economy in MexAmerica, an economy that belongs neither to the U.S. nor to the Third World, became apparent as early as the 1980s. In 1986, the lowest per capita incomes in the U.S. were in the Texas border cities of Brownsville-Harlingen, Laredo, and McAllen-Edinburg-Mission. Per capita incomes in all of these cities had fallen to less than half the national average for the U.S. Las Cruces, New Mexico, and El Paso, Texas, were but a notch above this depth, having per capita incomes that were, respectively, 65 and 65.4 percent of the U.S. average.[118]

The most significant economic development leading to the rise of Mex-America is the *maquiladora* or Border Industrialization Program; i.e., the promotion of a network of factories in Mexico but near the U.S. border.[119] The *maquiladora* program allows foreigners to have total ownership of factories in Mexico if their products are exported. (Other enterprises in Mexico must have Mexican ownership of at least 51 percent.) Obviously, the *maquiladora* program is most attractive to U.S. investors who can have products manufactured in Mexico as cheaply as they could in South Korea or Singapore, yet have the convenience of ease of transport of the finished products to U.S. markets.

Writing in 1989 in his *The New Realities,* economist Peter F. Drucker traced the theme of economic independence which runs throughout Mexico's history -- Juarez's attempt to keep the country Indian and rural, Porfirio Diaz's attempt to import European capital and expertise to counter the *Yanqui,* the more recent attempt to develop industrial self-sufficiency through a protected market -- but concluded that the survival of the nation -- divided as it is between an industrial, Spanish-speaking north and a rural, Indian south -- depends upon "abandonment of Mexico's century-old policy of economic independence and acceptance of economic integration with the United States."[120] Drucker notes the rapidly developing *maquiladora* movement, but asks, "will the United States be able, let alone willing, to accept economic integration when Mexican wages are one-tenth of American ones, and farm products grown on Mexican irrigated land south of the border cost one-third of what it costs to grow them north of the border?"[121]

By the beginning of the 1990s, an answer to Drucker's question had become apparent. Neither Mexico nor the United States, if taken in isolation as separate nations, would accept economic integration. Rather, it was to be realized gradually through the creation of the new third nation of Mex-America, which would be real enough as a geo-economic entity while having no existence in the law. MexAmerica would attract the low-wage labor of southern Mexico indefinitely, especially if free trade between the two nations led to the rise of a high-wage industrial belt running across northern Mexico. From there, the U.S. side of an increasingly inconsequential border would exert a further attraction.

Speaking to an interviewer from *The New York Times* in December, 1991, Wayne Cornelius concluded that "Free trade has been oversold as a quick fix to the immigration problem. Most people are focusing on two, three years . . . . You've got to think in terms of 10, 15, 20 years for a free trade agreement to have a demonstrably significant impact on the volume and kind of labor migration that is occurring between the two countries."[122]

"In the meantime," according to the *Times'* reporter, "new laws allowing Mexican peasants to sell their community lands, along with an expected end to the huge subsidies that Mexico pays its corn farmers, could propel some new immigrants northward. And it remains to be seen whether the factory and agriculture jobs that free trade might create in northern Mexico could actually foster illegal immigration by drawing people from southern Mexico and Central America to the edge of the United States."[123]

Even if fewer factories are built on the U.S. side of MexAmerica, its emergent service economy will exert an attraction for northward migration.

This new economy is ideally suited for low-wage immigrant labor. Saskia Sassen, an economist writing in 1990 in the *Journal of International Affairs* on "U.S. Immigration Policy Toward Mexico in a Global Economy," explains that "the transformation of the occupational and income structure in the United States -- itself in good part a result of the globalization of production -- has created an expanding supply of low-wage jobs. The decline of manufacturing and the growth of services have contributed to make more jobs temporary and part-time, reduced advancement opportunities within firms, and weakened various types of job protection. The resulting casualization of the labor market facilitates the absorption of immigrants, including undocumented immigrants."[124]

Sassen suggests that the merging of the economies of the U.S. and Mexico will take precedence over questions of immigration control because "These are powerful changes -- in the United States, in Mexico and in the conditions that bind the two countries. If we add to this the internationalization of many key markets and the growth of U.S. foreign investment, we must then ask whether a policy aimed at strict control of U.S. borders is viable or whether we should move towards a fundamental rethinking of the immigration question, one which would, for example, replace border control with protection of workers' wages and rights in both Mexico and the United States."[125]

Advocates of free trade usually maintain that industries in developing countries cannot compete with those of an advanced industrial nation because the low wages of the former are counterbalanced by their low productivity. In a report published in 1991 with U.S.-Mexican free trade in mind, Walter Russell Mead of the Economic Policy Institute pointed out that low productivity is not necessarily always present in low-wage economies.[126] If Mead's report is valid, it would seem that the *maquiladoras* combine the best of both economic worlds -- the low wages of the Third World, the high productivity of the First World -- at least, from the standpoint of those investing in them. It is appropriate to note that Japan, which has been adopting robotic production systems at a rate comparable to any other economy in the world, was among the first nations other than the U.S. to invest in *maquiladoras*.[127] Obviously, the combination of wages below even those of Asia and high productivity through the use of robotics is an appealing possibility, one which is increasingly being realized. MexAmerica, considered as an economic phenomenon, would seem to have a bright future.[128]

MexAmerica, however, is more than an economic phenomenon, a good investment for some people. Under the name of Aztlan, it is claimed as their homeland by the Chicano nationalists. Aztlan, they explain, was the name given by the Aztecs to the northern land from which they descended into Mexico to found the city of Tenochtitlan.[129] Today, however, it is a captive nation, subjugated and exploited by the *Yanqui* imperialists.

The name Aztlan was first given currency in 1969, when the Chicano National Liberation Youth Conference was held at Denver. The conference produced ''The Spiritual Plan of Aztlan,'' of which the following are typical passages:

> In the spirit of a new people that is conscious not only of its proud heritage, but also of the brutal ''gringo'' invasion of our territories, we, the Chicano inhabitants and civilizers of the northern land of Aztlan . . . declare that the call of our blood is . . . our inevitable destiny. Aztlan belongs to those who plant the seeds, water the fields, and gather the crops, and not to the foreign Europeans. We do not recognize capricious frontiers on the Bronze Continent . . . . We declare the independence of our mestizo Nation . . . . Before the world, before all of North America . . . we are a Nation. We are Aztlan.[130]

Partisans of Aztlan in following years contributed to the establishment of departments of Chicano Studies in colleges and universities. These in turn generated a literature in support of their aims. Typical of the revisionist histories produced is Rodolfo Acuna's *Occupied America: The Chicano's Struggle Toward Liberation,* which defends the thesis that ''The Mexican-American War was not only an unjust war but . . . it was just as brutal as the repression perpetuated by other colonial regimes. The Anglo-Texans' treatment of the Mexican was violent and often inhumane. The Anglo-American invasion of Mexico was as vicious as that of Hitler's invasion of Poland and other Central European nations, or, for that matter, U.S. involvement in Vietnam.''[131]

It is not clear whether most Chicano nationalists favor independence for Aztlan itself or seek its annexation by Mexico. If the latter, then the rise of Chicano separatism would introduce to Americans a problem new to the Western Hemisphere, but one that has long been known to Europe. This is irredentism, a term which, in the definition of Max H. Boehm, ''is derived from the Italian *irredenta* (unredeemed). The concept originated in the nineteenth century in connection with the Italian movement which, after the unification of Italy, aimed at the annexation of Italian-speaking regions still under Austrian or Swiss Rule, such as Trent, Dalmatia, Istria, Trieste and Fiume. The concept, however, has become detached from its concrete and specific connotation and has come to denote any movement which aims to unite politically with its co-national mother state a region under foreign rule.''[132]

The classic irredentist situation involves an area of one nation-state, adjacent or in proximity to another nation-state, which was formerly owned by the latter and has a majority of its inhabitants sharing the same ethnic identity as the latter. The demographic factor is the *sine qua non* of irredentism, but no less essential is the conviction, generally held by the citizens of at least one of the two nation-states, that the frontiers of nationality and of polity should coincide, that all nation-states should recognize "ethnicity" as the basis of citizenship, even if that involves rectifying historic "injustices" of decades or centuries past.

What "Anglos" see as Chicano separatism is, seen from a perspective south of the Rio Grande, Mexican irredentism. Since even *Yanqui* historians readily and perhaps unthinkingly "admit" that the U.S. "stole" the Southwest from Mexico, and since the moral and historical basis for an irredentist movement has already been established by Chicano authors, it would seem that the rise of Mexican irredentism as a serious political movement awaits only the demographic transformation of the Southwest.

Boehm notes three "counter-remedies for irredentist difficulties . . . : the rectification of frontiers, assimilation and accord of interests."[133] Resort to the first procedure as a formal, legal process seems to be of the highest order of improbability in the case of Mexican irredentism. The second is the officially expressed remedy offered by the governing stratum of the U.S. whenever American society is confronted with intergroup conflict. Increasingly, however, the third remedy is the one which will be attempted in practice, albeit that official expressions of public policy will continue to pay homage to the American ideal of *e pluribus unum*.

Rectification of frontiers following either a protracted guerrilla war or decades of chronic terrorism may, however, not be ruled out as an option by those who seek such rectification. The fact that such an effort is unlikely to be successful may not be sufficient to deter those who are fanatically committed to what they see as self-determination for their homeland. When the small band of enthusiasts following John Brown to Harper's Ferry were apprehended, their plot seemed almost ludicrous for the dimensions of the ambition which inspired it. Nonetheless, history demonstrated that Brown's raid was merely a harbinger of what was to come. Similarly, partisans of Aztlan may one day also choose to act, hoping that even a failed *Putsch* might lead to a later and successful uprising.

Something like this has already been planned, although it was not put into action. *El Plan de San Diego* has received much attention from Chicano historians. Alfredo Mirande describes it as follows in his *Gringo Justice:*

> . . . a Mexican national, Basilo Ramos, arrested by Starr County Sheriff Deodoro Guerra, was found to have in his possession a copy of an irredentist plan known as *El Plan de San Diego* because it was signed in San Diego, Texas. *El Plan* called for a general uprising on February 20, 1915, and declared independence from "Yankee tyranny." . . . This uprising was to be effected by a liberating army composed not only of Mexicans but blacks, Japanese, and Indians. The Indians were to have their land returned to them and several

southeastern states were designated for blacks. A new independent republic
was to be created from five southwestern states (i.e., Texas, New Mexico,
Arizona, Colorado, and California). Every white male over the age of 16 was to
be shot, as were all traitors who cooperated with the enemy.[134]

Writing in 1980 in *Aztlan: International Journal of Chicano Studies Research,* Douglas W. Richmond provides more details regarding *El Plan.*
According to Richmond, when the plan "did not attract armed support by the
announced date of the revolt, German agents and Mexican organizers in-
tervened to attempt some measure of success . . . . A revised plan . . . emphasized proletarian solidarity among the ethnic groups of Texas. It also
reemphasized the socialism of the original declaration so that Mexicans could
regain their lands under the traditional communal order."[135] Richmond believes that "In the beginning, the revolt seemed to have a high probability of
success,"[136] but "Undoubtedly the major reason for the defeat of the Plan de
San Diego was the ruthless response of local authorities. The murderous
assaults of the Rangers resulted in increased fighting because of Texas-style
ley fuga executions of those who were apprehended or merely suspected of
joining the revolt."[137]

The plan is noteworthy for its ideological sophistication. Its attempt to find
in Mexico's *ejidos,* or common lands, an agrarian base for a socialist revolution parallels Lenin's conviction that the Russian *mir,* or common lands,
would serve as a similar agrarian base for revolution in Russia. His discovery
of this pre-capitalist communalism led Marx to take a more favorable view of
Russia when, in 1882, he wrote a preface to the Russian translation of his
*Communist Manifesto.*[138] The presence of a similar primitive agrarian communalism in Mexico has led leftists since the time of John Reed to look
hopefully to that nation.

That leftists may not be wholly fatuous in placing their hopes in an Aztlan
strategy is suggested by the results of a survey taken in 1982, which reveal that
Mexicans were then as yet relatively untainted by "bourgeois individualism."
Asked if they agreed with the statement that "The individual owes his first
duty to the state and only secondarily to his personal welfare," citizens of
several nations answered as follows:

> United States — 25% yes; 68% no
> United Kingdom — 38% yes; 55% no
> West Germany — 41% yes; 45% no
> Italy — 48% yes; 32% no
> Mexico — 92% yes; 5% no[139]

Although the press read by Mexico's elite may not reflect this sense of primitive collectivism, it does speak for Mexican nationalism and irredentism. The following are excerpts from "The Great Invasion: Mexico Recovers Its Own," an article which appeared in 1982 in *Excelsior*, Mexico's leading daily newspaper:

> The U.S. upper classes in the Western states live in increasing splendor. Their apogee of luxury and comfort doubtlessly marks the inevitable beginning of their decadence. The Mexican invasion continues . . . .
>
> The territory lost in the XIX century by a Mexico torn by internal strife and under centralist dictatorships led by paranoid chiefs, like Antonio Lopez de Santa Anna, seems to be restoring itself through a humble people who go on settling various zones that once were ours on the old maps.
>
> Land, under any concept of possession, ends up in the hands of those who deserve it. All of us Mexicans should prove ourselves worthy of what we have and what we want. The problem is one of organization.[140]

*Excelsior* in 1986 conducted a survey of Mexicans' perceptions of the U.S. The results, as reported in *The Atlanta Constitution*, were as follows: "Fifty-nine percent of 550 people polled said the United States was 'an enemy country' when asked how they viewed Mexico's northern neighbor, compared with 31 percent who said the United States was 'a friendly country.' Ten percent of those polled did not answer."[141]

Irredentism is promoted not merely by private publications such as *Excelsior,* but also by the Mexican government. In 1981, the Mexican government opened the National Museum of Intervention, specifically intended for the education of youth. The following are excerpts from Larry Rohter's article in *The New York Times* regarding this rather unusual museum:

> At the entrance stands Uncle Sam, his ax raised triumphantly over a prostrate Mexico. But inside the National Museum of Intervention, the tables are turned, and it is the United States that comes under unrelenting attack.
>
> In the course of their history as neighbors, Mexico and the United States have endured relations often marked by tension, conflict and mutual suspicion. Nowhere in Mexico is that phenomenon more apparent than at this self-described "repository of national memory" maintained mainly for the benefit of the nation's schoolchildren.
>
> Housed in a former convent, the museum contains exhibits, maps, weapons, documents and photographs that convey a distinctly Mexican view of that uneasy relationship. Financed and administered by the Mexican government, the museum, inaugurated just before Mexican Independence Day in 1981, is both a monument to two centuries of accumulated rancor and an affirmation of national identity . . . .

Much of the museum focuses on the events leading up to and accompanying "the Mutilation," as the Treaty of Guadalupe Hidalgo is often called here. In that treaty, which followed the victory of the United States in the war of 1846-48, Mexico lost more than half its claimed territory, which became the American Southwest.

The deaths of Mexicans in that struggle for continental supremacy are referred to here as "exterminations" or "assassinations." American victims like the 365 combatants executed on Palm Sunday in 1836 after their surrender at what is now Goliad, Tex., are described, on the other hand, merely as having been "shot."[142]

While the Mexican government portrays the U.S. as an enemy of Mexico's people, it could be argued that some public officials in California, Texas, and Arizona have been, in fact, overly solicitous of their interests. A few exemplary instances are the following: Property owners in San Diego's McGonigle Canyon, confronted with illegal entrants squatting on their land, experienced difficulty in getting city authorities to enforce the laws against trespassing.[143] California's Assembly passed a resolution urging the federal government to delay building a ditch along the U.S.-Mexican border because the proposed ditch had aroused protests in Mexico when the governor opened the state's new trade office there.[144] A "Buy American-Buy Texan Bill," passed in the Texas legislature only after Mexico was defined in the bill as American.[145] Also approved was a bill to allow Mexican nationals to pay in-state tuition when they attend five Texas state universities in the border area.[146] San Antonio's Mayor Henry Cisneros, in an address delivered to Albuquerque's Hispano Chamber of Commerce, argued that "there is no way to seal the border."[147] Not to be outdone, Texas's Lieutenant Governor Bob Hobby called for open borders, explaining that "By an accident of history, a particular shallow river is now found to be a boundary and people crossing that river without getting a paper stamped are termed illegal immigrants and therefore thought to be some great problem."[148] Arizona's Governor Bruce Babbitt told LULAC (the League of United Latin American Citizens) that Mexico's debt to the U.S. should be halved because "The banks can soak it up."[149]

By the 1990s, MexAmerica had begun to evolve its own regional politics, a politics as unique as was that of the so-called Solid South prior to 1954. The American officials cited above, as well as others, had begun to pay an implicit obeisance to the new political realities of their region. Their compliant attitude may partially explain why the Chicano nationalists, unlike their predecessors in the late 1960s, had apparently elected "the long march through the institutions" as a strategy rather than militance.

At the end of the 1960s, there emerged a party which in type was new to American politics, albeit a type long-established in the politics of Old World multi-national states such as the Austro-Hungarian Empire. The plan of Aztlan had proclaimed ''Por La Raza todo, Fuera de la Raza nada'' and condemned ''the two-party system'' as ''the same animal with two heads that feed from the same trough.''[150] In answer to this call for an alternative, *La Raza Unida* Party was organized in Crystal City, Texas. A Chicano nationalist party, it nonetheless accepted enough of Marxism to win the sympathies of *Yanqui* leftists. The latter affected to believe that *La Raza Unida* meant ''the people united,'' despite the fact that Spanish language dictionaries invariably translate *la Raza* as *race* or *clan* or *breed.*[151]

Leading organizers of *La Raza Unida* were Rodolfo Gonzales, organizer of the Denver conference; Jose Gutierrez, of California's Mexican American Youth Organization; and Reies Tijerina, who had founded the at once militant and traditionalist *Alianza Federal de Mercedes* in 1963 to contest ownership of public lands in New Mexico and then to occupy them. Standing against assimilation and for self-determination, the candidates of *La Raza Unida* achieved some electoral success in several towns in southern Texas, but by 1972 the party had begun to decline.[152]

Chicano nationalists began their long march through the institutions in 1969, when the Chicano Coordinating Council on Higher Education met to issue ''El Plan de Santa Barbara.'' This plan was directed to the colleges and universities and called for the establishment of Chicano Studies programs. A student organization was also founded, the *Movimiento Estudiantil Chicano de Aztlan* or MECHA. With this development ended what Mario Barrera, in his *Beyond Aztlan: Ethnic Autonomy in Comparative Perspective,* calls ''the classic period'' of the Chicano movement. This combined both ''communitarian and egalitarian goals under the ideological label of Chicanismo.''[153]

In the following years, according to Barrera, the movement ''fragmented and diverged,'' often neglecting the communitarian goal in its pursuit of socio-economic and political equality.[154] The August Twenty-Ninth Movement, however, kept alive the hope of independence for Aztlan. According to Barrera, ''The ATM based its position on certain concepts Lenin and Stalin had developed to deal with the political problem of multiple ethnic groups in Russia and Eastern Europe . . . . The key concept here was that of national self-determination, which meant that any group that met certain criteria of 'nationhood' was free to determine its own national boundaries, even if that meant seceding from an existing state.''[155]

Barrera believes that the Chicano movement in the 1990s is regaining sight of its communitarian goal, especially since American society has begun to evolve towards multiculturalism. His *Beyond Aztlan* might well serve as a *vade mecum* for that movement. It is well-documented, closely argued, and scholarly in tone, avoiding the stentorian rhetoric which characterized ''El Plan'' in its previous appearances.

Although American society has held that an ethnic group can achieve equality only by losing its distinctive collective identity, Barrera points to "a tradition of thought in the United States that supports the concept of a pluralistic accommodation . . . . This is the cultural pluralism position, originally expounded by the Jewish philosopher Horace Kallen."[156]

Kallen, surveying the nation's cultural pluralism in 1924, insisted that "the cultural outcome" will be "not the melting pot. Rather something that becomes more and more distinct in the changing state and city life of the last two decades, and which is most articulate and apparent among just those peoples whom the sociologists and Americanizers are most accustomed to praise -- the Scandinavians, the Germans, the Irish, the Jews."[157] Kallen noted that each of these nationalities predominated in the population of a different area of the U.S. -- Scandinavians in Minnesota, Germans in the Midwest, Irish in Massachusetts, Jews in a large section of New York City -- and concluded that these areas should be developed as nations within the nation, taking Switzerland as a model. Kallen rejected the possibility of assimilation because "In historic times . . . no new ethnic types have originated, and there comes no assurances that the old types will disappear in favor of the new."[158]

Barrera believes, however, that cultural pluralism has "remained a curiously incomplete intellectual concept" in contemporary America, where it seems to be simply "a supportive set of attitudes." He believes, however, that "regional autonomy" is necessary because

A more realistic analysis would take note . . . that culture is rooted in and shaped by a whole range of institutions: the mass media, which transmit cultural attitudes in a very direct manner; the schools, with their impact on language learning; the corporations, which reward certain types of language skills and cultural attributes and penalize others; the government, which is a major employer itself and which sets policies affecting all of the other institutions. As the Quebecois well know, a "do-your-own-thing-on-your-own-time" attitude doesn't take you very far toward cultural pluralism if everyone knows that English is the only way to get ahead. To achieve a real rather than an illusory cultural pluralism, then, requires a set of supportive institutions, such as are found in Quebec and Switzerland but not in the United States.[159]

Barrera defines regional autonomy as "a kind of in-between solution to ethnic and nationalist demands, poised between separatism and secession on the one hand and assimilation without choice on the other."[160] Ironically, the nations which Barrera sees as models for the attainment of this ideal -- Canada, Switzerland, and Belgium -- are precisely those cited in the warnings of Governor Lamm and others. What is a disaster for one party appears to be an ideal compromise or accord, the third of Boehm's counter-remedies, to the other.

What Lamm and others see as an extreme solution, Barrera defines as "implicit regional autonomy. In both Canada and Switzerland, a federal system of government has combined with the coexistence of different ethnic groups to produce a system of ethnic regional autonomy that is not called by that name."[161] Explicit regional autonomy exists in China and, when Barrera was writing, in Nicaragua where the Sandinista government sought to appease the Moskito Indians.[162]

Hannum and Lillich, writing in *The American Journal of International Law* on the concept of autonomy, provide Barrera with a legal model. Hannum and Lillich's definition of "the *minimum* governmental powers that a territory would need to possess if it were to be considered fully autonomous" resembles American federalism. The powers enumerated, all subject to the principal government, include "a locally elected body with some legislative power," "a locally chosen chief executive," and "an independent local judiciary." Also, "the status of autonomy and at least partial self-government is not inconsistent with the denial of any local authority over specific areas of special concern to the principal/sovereign government" and is also "consistent with power-sharing arrangements between the central and autonomous governments."[163]

At first glance, and admittedly without reading the fine print, this legal model seems to be a replica of the American federal system. The crucial difference, however, is that such a regional government would be implicitly or explicitly conducted in the name of a specific ethnic group. This difference, moreover, involves a matter of content, not of form.

Barrera recognizes the practical difficulty that "ethnic groups overlap in their patterns of residence, so that it is not possible to draw neat boundaries around regions. This is the type of argument that the Quebecois call mappism." The answer to "mappism" is China, where "one ethnic group lives in the valleys and another on the ridges of hills, and so on."[164]

Demographic trends, Barrera believes, favor the rise of ethnic autonomy areas. He cites the demographic studies of Bouvier, the Southern California Association of Governments, and others to conclude that "the most likely candidates for Chicano regional autonomy areas are southern California, northern New Mexico, and southern Texas."[165] Chicanos either have majorities or will have majorities of the populations in these areas. In New Mexico, their roots go back four centuries.

It is impossible to predict whether or not Barrera's plan will be realized, but he notes that "no one predicted the Chicano Movement, nor the Quiet Revolution in Canada." The latter revolution was spearheaded by "intellectuals and professionals" when "a rising strata of Quebecois professionals and administrators found their path blocked by the established order with its ethnic stratification system." A similar movement could arise among Chicano intellectuals and professionals "now there are Chicano journals, Chicano Studies programs, and a National Association for Chicano Studies, as well as a host of professional organizations."[166]

Implementation of Barrera's plan could follow one of the two following models:

> One is the explicit model, which would require the designation of special areas specifically for ethnic autonomy, and would be a modification of the existing federal system. The other route would be to work for the redrawing of state lines, carving out new states that would have a majority or plurality Chicano population. This route would be more along the Canadian or Swiss model, in that it would not necessarily require a change in existing federal principles . . . . In passing, it might be noted that the idea of dividing California into more than one state is not a new idea. In the years prior to 1915, many such efforts originated in southern California. Since then, a number of others have come from the northern part of the state.[167]

The explicit model seems to be outrageously improbable. Something approaching it, however, has already been attempted. In 1985, an Arizona state legislator proposed a state resolution to prohibit "Persons who do not speak a native language indigenous to the region, or who are not descendants of persons living in the area prior to the [Gadsden] purchase from residing in the territory acquired under the Gadsden Purchase Act of 1853."[168] The area of the Gadsden Purchase includes the southern third of Arizona. While the attempt failed in 1985, and would undoubtedly have been quashed by the federal courts, it is significant that such an attempt was even made.

The second model is also not as improbable as it seems. Although the U.S. Constitution requires approval by Congress of the creation of new states from old states, and although such approval would seem to be unlikely to be given since such a new state would have two new Senators, attempts to create new states by secession from the old are not unknown. In November, 1980, voters in five of six counties in south New Jersey approved a non-binding referendum which sought approval to initiate a political process toward separate statehood for "South Jersey."[169] Advocates of a new state of South Jersey have long felt alienated from ethnically different Newark, which dominates the northern part of the state. A similar estrangement from Detroit has moved some people in northern and peninsular Michigan to seek independence from southern Michigan.

The Republic of Texas, in the treaty admitting it to the U.S., reserved the right to divide itself into five states. Donald Whisenhunt, a Texas historian, has published a book, *The Five States of Texas: An Immodest Proposal* (Austin, Tex.: Eakin Press, 1987), arguing that Texas should claim this right.

Many Texas legislators might well be tempted to claim the right of Texas to be divisible, if only to rid themselves of the burden imposed by "the Texas-Mexico border region -- an area that costs the state twice as much as it generates in tax revenues."[170]

Stan Statham introduced in the California Assembly, as soon as it convened in 1992, a bill to create a new state from the 27 northernmost counties of California. There was no evidence that Statham's move was a pre-emptive one aimed against Chicano nationalism, but *The New York Times* reported that "Since the secession plan came to light, many people here have suggested that it is a barely disguised effort by the politically conservative, nearly all-white rural counties to disassociate themselves from cities known for celebrating their ethnic and cultural diversity." Evidence that Statham truly reflected the sentiments of his constituents was forthcoming when voters in the 27 northern counties voted overwhelmingly in favor of a secession measure which was added to the June 1992 primary ballot.[171]

The "worst-case" scenario in the Southwest and elsewhere in the United States may well prove to be not the secession of an ethnic enclave, but the development, hastened by a period of crisis, of quasi-independent city-states and new states, each of which would claim for itself a kind of *imperium in imperio,* while not disdaining to receive more than its share of the federal revenue. Acceptance of this arrangement would be the price paid for civil peace or for securing the territory in question from occupation by the troops of a foreign power, one congenial to the area's inhabitants or even seen by them as their true homeland. It is not inconceivable that a day may dawn on the U.S. when a curious reversal will have taken place in which States' Rights, from having been the last resort of reactionaries, will have become the favored strategy of revolutionaries.

# IV

# *Government as Conflict Management*

A lthough Canada, Switzerland, and Belgium are cautionary examples for Governor Lamm, they are praiseworthy examples for Mario Barrera. Attempting to approach them from a value-free stance, one finds that all three are primarily examples of government as conflict management. Government as conflict management is an emerging theme of public life in the U.S., a theme which recurrently manifests itself in the concepts of dialogue, mediation, sensitivity, tolerance, and balance. The latter terms are increasingly the shibboleths of American public life. The fiction is maintained that these concepts, somehow infused into the governing process, will produce a final resolution of intergroup conflicts. Despite all the verbal obeisance which is paid to the ideal of conflict resolution, the reality is something quite other. The reality is that, as American society as a whole follows the way of Miami and of Monterey Park, conflicts become chronic. Conflict management, therefore, is becoming an ongoing, never-ending process, a prerequisite to governance itself.

Canada provides the most instructive example for the U.S. because of its similar political system. For this reason, it may provide a forecast of the fate for the U.S. political system if the U.S. develops an ethnic mix as problematic as that which exists in Canada. The problematic nature of the Canadian ethnic mix is the fact that the ethnic majority has an insufficiently large majority, while the ethnic minority enjoys the leverage of geographical concentration. In 1986, of Canada's approximately 25 million citizens, about 62 percent had English as their mother tongue and 25 percent French, while 16 percent were bilingual. Eighty percent of the 6,540,000 citizens of Quebec spoke French. Significant concentrations of French-speakers were also to be found in adjacent provinces.[172]

The political system of modern Canada originated with the British North America Act of 1867. Since Canada faces the threat of dissolution through the secession of its French-speaking region, it is ironic that the Act of 1867 was written with reference to the cautionary example of the U.S. According to Michael Rush, writing in *The USA and Canada 1990,* a yearbook in the Europa series,

> The discussions and negotiations between the various British colonies leading to the creation of the Dominion of Canada were conducted during, and in the aftermath of, the American Civil War, and the widespread Canadian view was that too much power had been assigned to the states in the U.S. system, thus rendering that system unstable, vulnerable to secession and lacking central direction. The Canadian politicians therefore sought to establish a federal union which was as centralized as circumstances and opinion would allow, with minimal concessions to provincial and regional sensibilities.[173]

Despite this strong, centralized government, Canada has moved steadily during the late twentieth century towards an official division into at least two separate societies. This is evidence for the maxim of Charles Maurras that the legal nation should not be confused with the real nation. The real (ethnic) nation of Canada has been divided from its beginning. This reality finally penetrated through the old legalities of 1867 when, in 1982, the Constitution Act was passed which states that the Canadian Charter of Rights and Freedoms "shall be interpreted in a manner consistent with the preservation and enhancement of the multicultural heritage of Canadians."[174] In June 1987, the Meech Lake Accord further recognized a "distinct status" for Quebec as a "distinct French-speaking society." The Accord was an act of accommodation designed to secure Quebec's acceptance of the new Constitution.[175]

These two great concessions, among others from "English" Canada, were granted after two decades of French separatist activity which began in earnest when the *Parti Quebecois* was founded in 1967. Like *La Raza Unida,* the *Parti Quebecois* at first limited its electoral efforts to local elections, where victories were most likely. By 1976, the party was able to wrest control of the provincial government away from the Liberals. In 1980, it placed before the voters a proposal for "sovereignty association," which, if approved, would have granted political autonomy to Quebec while retaining a close economic association with Canada. Although the vote on the referendum went against the separatists, it did so largely because of the opposition of the English-speaking minority within Quebec.[176] The rise of the *Parti Quebecois* to power and its displacement of the Liberals was, however, an irreversible victory for separatism because, for the first time, the real nation (as embodied in an ethnically based party) had triumphed over the legal nation (as represented by a party standing for a universalist ideology).

A popular theory regarding the sudden rise of Quebec separatism holds that it was generated by dissatisfaction with economic disparities between the two major ethnic groups. It is often true that economic inequalities which are accepted within an ethnic group become insufferable between ethnic groups, particularly if there is no rationale for the distinction which is accepted by all groups involved. According to this theory, conflict has arisen in Quebec from "a clear cultural division of labor" in which Francophones were left at the lower levels of income in the province's major corporations, most of which were owned by Anglophones.[177]

If outrage over this inequality provided an impetus for Quebec separatism, that fact bodes ill for the Southwest U.S., where a similar two-tier structure of incomes has long existed. Although the gap in incomes may be closing in the U.S., as it has been in Quebec, this movement towards ethnic parity often, paradoxically, leads to a revolution of rising expectations rather than to a long-term accommodation. This fact would explain the presence in the Quebec separatist movement of numerous young white collar and professional workers.

Even a movement towards linguistic assimilation may have effects other than those anticipated by the conventional wisdom. The fear that French was slowly being displaced as a language of the majority in certain strategic areas of Quebec led to a strong separatist reaction. The fact that Montreal was, in 1971, only 60 percent French-speaking and that immigrants were overwhelmingly choosing English as their preferred language acted as a catalyst for a pro-French reaction.[178]

Francophones counterattacked by passing in the Quebec provincial legislature Bills 22 and 101, which required use of French in the workplace, advertising in French, and attendance in French schools for children of immigrants not from an English-speaking background.[179] In 1974, Quebec declared itself unilingual, in clear violation of the 1867 Constitution. "English" Canada attempted to accommodate Quebec's Francophones to the extent that "in Ontario, which is 5% French-speaking, drivers' licences and other official documents are printed in French and English; in Quebec, which is 20% English-speaking, such documents are printed in French only."[180]

In a nine-year period following the triumph of the *Parti Quebecois* in 1976, no less than 200,000 Anglophones chose to leave the province. In mid-1991, a poll revealed that "nearly a third of the remaining 800,000 Anglophones in Quebec plan to leave within five years because of what they perceive as growing restrictions on the use of their language . . . . The same surveys indicate that if Quebec separated from Canada, 44 percent would leave."[181]

The Meech Lake Accord may prove to have been the last attempt at accommodation on the part of "English" Canada. In the months following its failure, when Newfoundland and Manitoba refused to ratify the Accord, separatist sentiment in Quebec reached new heights. According to a survey taken in 1990, ''66 percent of Quebeckers support sovereignty-association . . . . If non-French residents are excluded, Franco-Quebeckers favoring sovereignty-association are about 80 percent, with 70 percent for independence.''[182]

By 1992, Quebec separatism had wholly transformed the national political system of Canada. The old bipartisan system of Progressive Conservatives and Liberals had been supplemented in the 1980s by the rise of the socialist New Democrats. The new party, however, like the older two, claimed to represent all of the nation while expressing sympathy with separatists' claim to belong to a repressed minority. The Quebec separatists, entering national politics as the *Bloc Quebecois,* created by reaction a new party in their mirror image. This latter was the Reform Party, leading in popularity all other parties in the western provinces. Followers of the Reform Party, mostly English-speaking evangelical Protestants, constituted a second ethnic party, one which also favored Quebec's secession, although for different reasons.

The power of the new ethnically driven politics of Canada was demonstrated strikingly in the results of the October, 1993, election. The Conservatives, who as recently as 1984 had held 211 seats in Parliament, won only two seats. The Reform Party won 52 seats, only two of which were won east of Saskatchewan, while the *Bloc Quebecois* won 54 seats, all in Quebec. The Liberals, with a majority of 178 seats, most of which were won in Ontario, faced the challenge of governing an ethnically and geographically polarized nation.[183]

In 1991, the separatist government of Quebec called for more accommodation from ''English'' Canada. The alternative was for Quebec to hold another referendum on ''sovereignty-association,'' a referendum which would probably be won by the separatists. Suggested solutions to Canada's constitutional crisis, short of either ''sovereignty-association'' or complete independence for Quebec, included a more decentralized federation or a confederation of regions or a ''bipolar'' federation in which Quebec would wield a veto power over national policy. Even these restructurings, however, would raise the question of Quebec's responsibility for the $380 billion of national debt; Quebec's role in any monetary union, given ''English'' Canada's reluctance to share control of the banking system; and Quebec's participation in any U.S.-Canadian free trade agreement.[184]

The secession of Quebec would leave the remainder of Canada in a dismembered condition. The maritime provinces -- New Brunswick, Newfoundland, Nova Scotia, and Prince Edward Island -- would be separated from the rest of Canada and might seek statehood within the U.S. These provinces, however, have had chronically depressed economies, costing Ottawa more in taxes than they have returned, and might not be welcomed as new states.[185]

The western provinces -- British Columbia, Alberta, Saskatchewan, and Manitoba -- have their own separatist movements. Some separatists seek an independent nation of Western Canada; others, union with the U.S. Western separatists, upon occasion, have elected members to their provincial legislatures. The example of an independent Quebec would increase separatist sentiment in a region which is geographically and economically distant from Ottawa.[186]

There are also separatist movements *within* provinces. The *Parti Acadien* seeks an autonomous Acadian province to be formed from the northern half of New Brunswick, where the French-speaking Acadians, who believe themselves to be distinct from the Quebecois, constitute the majority of the population.[187] In Nova Scotia, many Cape Bretoners also seek a separate province.[188] The Dene of the Northwest Territories see themselves as a distinct people and "nation," but seek only "independence and self-determination within the country of Canada." In the eastern portion of the Northwest Territories, some of the Inuit have sought union with the Greenlanders who, in turn, are seeking independence from Denmark.[189] In December 1991, Canada reached an accord with the Inuit, giving them mineral rights and a cash settlement of one billion dollars.[190]

An independent Quebec itself might be confronted by separatists boring from within. Edouard Cloutier, a University of Montreal political scientist, advised leaders of the *Parti Quebecois* meeting in 1991, in the words of *Maclean's,* "to consider establishing a military force to counter possible acts of sabotage and disorder from equally secessionist-minded groups -- natives and anglophones in particular." Desmond Morton, a historian speaking for the Canadian Institute of Strategic Studies, was quoted as warning that "I don't believe -- and here I disagree with *PQ* Leader Jacques Parizeau -- that countries break up easily or in a civilized way." Similarly, Barry Cooper, a University of Calgary political scientist, warned that "Not only is armed conflict possible, it is highly probable."[191]

"Native Canadians" are quite vocal in threatening secession from an independent Quebec. Bill Wilson, political secretary of the Assembly of First Nations, warned that "If we don't sit down and talk now, the confrontation will be 100 times as bad as it needs to be." Armed Mohawks had already confronted Quebec authorities at Oka in the summer of 1990. Ovide Mercredi, grand chief of the Assembly, has warned that the Cree will secede from Quebec should the province secede from Canada.[192]

Anglophones in Quebec are also more or less threatening. In sparsely populated northwestern Quebec, Anglophones constitute a majority of the population and argue that they belong with Ontario. *Maclean's* notes several works by historians and legal scholars who all maintain that a secessionist Quebec could not rightfully claim the boundaries granted to it in 1867.[193]

*Maclean's* further reports that Quebec's Anglophones were, in 1991, beginning to join Option Canada in its campaign "dedicated to carving a new province out of southwestern Quebec -- including the western half of the island of Montreal -- where most of the province's non-French-speaking population resides." Alliance Quebec proposes the formation of several such "English territories," while the Equality Party asks for a local option by which "electoral ridings voting against sovereignty in any future referendum should be allowed to form new provinces or join neighboring ones."[194]

Foremost among apparent exceptions to the rule that multinational states are torn by internal conflict is Switzerland, where three nationalities have lived under parliamentary democracy since 1648. This feat of ethnic balance is, however, more one of show than of substance. German, spoken in 1983 by 4.1 million of Switzerland's citizens, is the dominant language in 19 of the nation's 25 cantons, while French, spoken by 1.13 million, prevails in five, and Italian, spoken by 744,000, in only one. (The remaining 50,400 of the Swiss speak Romansch, a linguistic hybrid of German and Italian.)[195] Even with the predominance of one nationality, the Germans, Switzerland has maintained its political unity only by extending to its minorities "rights" or "entitlements" out of proportion to their percentages of the population.[196] Hans Kohn, the eminent historian of nationalism, cites Switzerland as an example of those multi-national states in which unity is maintained through a strategic surrender of the majority's right to rule to a minority's demand for compensatory perquisites. He concludes that

> Fundamental for the solution of problems of duo- or polyethnic states is not primarily the attitude of the minority or minorities but that of the majority. The weaker groups in the population must receive a greater consideration than would be proportional to their numerical strength. They must have a greater share in the benefits of the state than is their "due." Then they will know that the state is their homeland, too, and the natural privilege inherent in greater numbers or greater wealth will be compensated by "favors" extended to "the minority."[197]

As admirable as the peaceful and progressive land of the Swiss may be, one must yet ask if the compromises of majority rule that they have accepted to sustain an appearance of national unity do not so weaken the powers inherent in a nation-state's sovereignty as to render doubtful the strength of that superficial unity. Switzerland, a synthetic nation compounded of the *irredenta* of three neighboring nations, has probably endured only through the indifference of those neighbors rather than through any inner cohesion. Switzerland's unity has remained untested in the age of nationalism because it has not been invaded since 1515 by any neighboring nation.

Small in both population and area, Switzerland's unity has never been subjected to the internal structural stresses to which a large nation is subject. It has been able to afford the complex apparatus for "conflict resolution" which Juerg Steiner has described in his *Amicable Agreement Versus Majority Rule: Conflict Resolution in Switzerland.*[198] One must suspect that any attempt to transfer that apparatus of conflict resolution to the U.S., a nation fifty times larger, would result in a corresponding growth of bureaucracy at some exponential rate quite beyond a mere manifold of fifty.

Some evidence suggests that Switzerland has avoided internal conflict for a reason other than the accommodation to minority interests which Kohn cites. Arend Lijphart, a political scientist specializing in the study of plural societies, concludes that "One important factor in the explanation of political stability in religiously and linguistically heterogeneous Switzerland is that many of the cantons, where much of the country's decentralized politics take place, are quite homogeneous."[199] In indirect corroboration of Lijphart's thesis, it may be noted that political instability in recent years has emerged in one canton, Bern, in which a French-speaking, Catholic minority found its interests threatened by a German-speaking, Protestant majority. The *Rassemblement Jurassien* was formed by the Francophone minority, agitated more or less violently, and finally succeeded in bringing about the establishment in 1979 of a new, wholly French canton of Jura.[200]

Emerich K. Francis, in his *Interethnic Relations: An Essay in Sociological Theory,* recounts the history of cantonal division in Switzerland and concludes that ". . . for reasons that have no parallel anywhere else, Switzerland, contrary to common opinion, does not fit the model of a multiethnic nation-state. Accordingly, the manner in which their so-called national problems have been solved or circumvented does not permit a more general application."[201]

Belgium offers another example of the costs of conflict resolution. In 1989, of its total population of approximately ten million, 58 percent were Dutch-speaking Flemings and 32 percent French-speaking Walloons. Approximately a tenth of the population was bilingual and slightly less than one percent spoke German[202] Ethnic animosities were exacerbated from the nation's founding in 1830 because its capital, Brussels, was and is a French-speaking enclave in its Dutch-speaking northern half. Bias against the Flemings in education and government arose because, according to the political scientist Anthony Mughan, "Belgian elites, regardless of their region of origin or residence, had long embraced the French language and culture with the result that Flemish had become the language of the largely rural poor and powerless."[203] Belgium proved no exception to the truism that socio-economic differences that are accepted among occupational groups become insufferable when they are associated with ethnic groups. Chronic civil strife and political extremism was the result.[204]

Attempts to resolve this conflict have followed a route of accommodation that, if followed further, as seems likely, will ultimately lead to the abolition of the nation-state of Belgium. In 1962, a linguistic frontier was drawn between the nation's Flemish north and its Wallonian south. As conflict continued, the legal separation was accentuated with amendments to the Belgian Constitution in 1970 and 1971 which established three regions and two cultural councils, followed by the enactment in 1974 of legislation on "preparatory regionalization."[205] Devolution, the nearest approach yet to the actual division of Belgium into two separate nations, was implemented in 1980. According to a description of the enabling legislation which appeared in *The Economist*, it "aims to devolve power from the central government in Brussels to the two warring provinces -- though it looks like creating a five-tier government and a vastly complicated new bureaucracy in the process."[206] The five tiers comprise the following: (1) King, Parliament, and the already existing central bureaucracy; (2) a new Senate of 236 members to supplement the already existing Chamber of Deputies; (3) a Flemish regional council, having 118 members; a Brussels regional council, having 48 members; a Walloon regional council, having 70 members; (4) a Dutch-speaking council, having the 118 members of the Flemish regional council; a French-speaking council, having the 70 Walloon regional council members and all Brussels regional council members who speak French; (5) finally, a new legal institution (and one doubtless much needed in the new dispensation!), the Arbitration Court, having six Dutch-speaking and six French-speaking members.[207]

In the 1991 parliamentary elections, no less than 39 different political groups vied for representation. The largest gains in votes were realized by the Flemish Bloc, a nationalist party advocating a separate Flemish state and the resettlement of immigrants in their countries of origin.[208]

The irony of Belgium is that while it has produced many spokesmen for European unity, it is itself approaching geopolitical dissolution. According to political scientists Alain Genot and David Lowe, more Belgians each year have come to favor "a total separation between Flanders and Wallonia. In this perspective, even the 'economic and monetary union' which politicians strive for in the European Community would be abandoned in Belgium. A customs union, it is argued, would be sufficient as any closer link would inevitably be at the expense of the Flemish community."[209]

# V

# *When Conflict Management Fails*

I n Canada, Switzerland, and Belgium, the strategy of conflict management among contending ethnic blocs has had a measure of success, albeit at an incalculable cost in political integrity. Conflict management, early in the 1990s, was also being attempted as a strategy in Eastern Europe in general and in the Balkan states in particular. There, however, it seemed to be no more successful than it was from 1918 to 1940, the last period when these states, liberated from the Austro-Hungarian, Russian, and Ottoman empires, were left to their own devices. The apparent inter-ethnic calm within these nations after 1945 was, of course, one imposed by the authoritarian policies of the Soviet Union.

At first glance, the failure of conflict management in these states might seem to be due to their lack of a liberal democratic heritage, an important historical factor setting them apart from Canada, Switzerland, and Belgium. Other factors, however, may play an equally significant role. Not only are the contending ethnic groups in the Balkan states more culturally distant from one another than are the contending ethnic groups in Canada, Switzerland, and Belgium, but their geographic distribution is different and more problematic. Both of these factors are present or developing in the United States as well, indicating that a more likely model for its future, given a continuation of current trends, is to be found in the Balkan states.

Conflict in the Balkan states in this century begins with the demise of the Austro-Hungarian Empire in 1918. It is a little-known fact that the dissolution of the Habsburg state was as much due to a demographic shift prior to 1918 as it was to the upheavals associated with World War I. Preceding the empire's collapse was a great migration of Slavic-speaking subjects from its eastern regions into the culture-region dominated by German speakers. William H.

McNeill, a historian at the University of Chicago, describes this pattern of migration, as follows:

> Peasant migrants into the towns of Bohemia and Hungary had long been accustomed to learn German, and in a few generations became German in sentiment as well as in language. This process began to falter in the nineteenth century. When the number of Slav- and Magyar-speaking migrants living in the cities of the monarchy passed a certain point, newcomers no longer had to learn German for everyday life. Presently nationalist ideals took root and made a German identity seem unpatriotic. The result was that Prague became a Czech- and Budapest a Magyar-speaking city within half a century.[210]

Vienna was almost transformed by the same migration. According to Victor L. Tapie's *The Rise and Fall of the Habsburg Monarchy*, "Many Czechs left their country to look for work in the imperial capital. Around 1880, one-third of the population of Vienna, . . . consisted of Czech nationals."[211]

Under the Habsburgs, assimilation was tantamount to Germanization. When the Slavs and Magyars had increased in their numbers to the point where they could live without submitting to Germanization, they began their own process of reverse assimilation. The argument that progress, entry into a more highly industrialized culture, meant acceptance of Germanization had lost its appeal. Having the best of both worlds, the benefits of life in the German-speaking world and the comfort of life with one's own ethnic kin, had become possible.

The immediate outcome of this reverse assimilation was a demand for governmental devolution. (A more delayed outcome was a nationalistic reaction among the Germans in Austria.) The leaders of the non-German minorities, in the words of Emerich Francis, "demanded that the whole country be divided . . . into administrative subunits in such a way that each nationality [might] enjoy political autonomy at least on a local and regional level."[212] Others among their demands, for "review boards and courts of appeal" and for schools teaching in their native languages,[213] are already familiar phenomena in the U.S.

The demise of the Austro-Hungarian government has been described by Arnold Toynbee as follows:

> The Hapsburg Monarchy spent the last century of its existence in attempts -- all doomed to failure -- at hindering the inevitable revision of the map on national-ist lines . . . . By accepting the Austro-Hungarian *Ausgleich* of 1867 and its Austro-Polish corollary in Galicia, it succeeded in identifying its own interests with the national interests of the Magyar and Polish as well as the German elements in its dominions. But it would not or could not come to terms with its Roumanians and Czechoslovaks and Jugoslavs, and the pistol-shots of Sara-

jevo proved the signal for its obliteration from the map.[214]

W.N. Medlicott has offered this epitome of the Habsburgs' failure: "If the empire was to survive it must win the tolerance of the nationalities, but the nationalities had no tolerance towards one another."[215]

Among the successor states to the Austro-Hungarian Empire, the republic of Czechoslovakia seemed to be the most stable. Under the leadership of Tomas Masaryk, Czechoslovakia seemed to be a model of liberal democracy. Its division under German occupation was, according to all appearances, wholly the fault of the Germans, not the Czechs. The restoration of Czechslovakia as one state in 1945 seemed to be permanent, albeit that it was under the domination of the Soviet Union.

The withdrawal of Soviet influence in 1990 proved, however, that Czechoslovakian unity had always been more appearance than reality. A movement to partition Czechoslovakia began anew when the legislature met to drop the word Socialist from the country's official name. Czech legislators wanted the nation's new name to be the Czechoslovak Federative Republic, while the Slovaks wanted it to be Czecho-Slovak Republic. An official compromise, which allowed the use of the hyphen in Slovakia but not in the Czech territories of Bohemia and Moravia, seemed to satisfy no one. Slovaks noted that of the 538 employees of the Czechoslovakian president, Vaclav Havel, only five were Slovaks, a glaringly obvious underrepresentation of the Slovaks' third of the total population.[216] The failure of all attempts at conciliation, culminating in 1992 in the Slovaks' rejection of a federative pact, made the secession of Slovakia inevitable.[217]

The division of Czechoslovakia would seem to be easily accomplished, given the fact that its two major population groups are geographically separate. In Czechoslovakia, though, as in the Balkan states proper, the ethnic situation is more complex than is immediately apparent. A glance at the ethnic maps in the U.S. Central Intelligence Agency's *Atlas of Eastern Europe* reveals that the seemingly simple (west/east=Czech/Slovak) ethnic division is complicated by the presence of a Hungarian minority, 3.8 percent of the total population, settled along the southern boundary of Slovakia.[218] It is likely, therefore, that Slovakia will not be independent for long before it is confronted by Hungarian irredentism.

Returning Slovakia's Hungarians to a Greater Hungary may not be too difficult, but the "Hungarian problem" of the Romanians looks almost insoluble. Of Romania's 23.3 million people in 1990, 7.8 percent were Hungarians, most of whom were concentrated in an area surrounded by Romanians.[219] The decline of Marxism in Romania has been paralleled by the rise of inter-ethnic tensions and serious outbreaks of violence. The situation of the Gypsies or Romany folk, which was unenviable under the regime of

Nicolai Ceausescu, remained almost unchanged under the post-Marxist government.[220]

Bulgaria's total population of 8.9 million included in 1990 a minority (8.5 percent) of ethnic Turks.[221] The Turks were largely concentrated along the southern boundary of Bulgaria, just over the border from European Turkey. Years before Marxism began its decline in Bulgaria, the ethnic Turks were subjected to repressive laws which led hundreds of thousands of them to flee to Turkey. Ethnic Turks were only half as numerous in Bulgaria in 1990 as they were as recently as 1984. Although the exodus of the Turks adversely affected the Bulgarian economy, the Bulgarians seemed to be unrelenting in their campaign to expel them.[222]

Ethnic conflict has become most evident in Yugoslavia, where, during 1992, it escalated into civil war and led to the secession of several of the six component republics that were brought together in a unitary state in 1948. The death of Tito and the withdrawal of the Soviet threat to Yugoslavia's independence removed the last forces which compelled political unity. Paul Lendvai, writing in *International Affairs,* states that "The developments that have surprised so many by their dramatic violence can only make sense if the historical dimension is taken into account. The starting point is the long and widely suppressed fact that Yugoslavia is a country without Yugoslavs. That is, it lacks people prepared to declare themselves as belonging to a Yugoslav entity as opposed to a specific nationality. According to the last census in 1981, only 1.2 million people out of a total population of 22.4 million described themselves as Yugoslavs."[223]

At 5.4 percent of the total population of 23.8 million in 1990, persons designating themselves as Yugoslavs were outnumbered by Serbs (36 percent), Croats (20 percent), Slovenians (9 percent), Muslims (8 percent), and Albanians (6 percent).[224] Yugoslavs in Yugoslavia were, in fact, little more than a legal fiction. As Lendvai explains, "They were primarily partners in or children of so-called 'mixed marriages' between, for example, Croats and Serbs or Slovenes and Macedonians. Others were army officers and NCOs, civil servants and diplomats."[225]

The United States of America may one day be without Americans to the same degree that Yugoslavia is without Yugoslavs. This parallel between the two countries is striking. The people who tell the U.S. Census Bureau that they are simply "Americans," a still significant minority, are mostly descendants of two or more European nationalities. The U.S. also has a small group of professed Americans who may not be of mixed ancestry, but who, as in the case of the minority of official Yugoslavs, either belong to governing circles or are their civil servants. Many of the professed Americans are, like the professed Yugoslavs, only players of a role in a sham show of national unity.

When, in a matter of months, the illusion of Yugoslavian unity began to vanish, some thoughtful observers dared to draw parallels between the two countries. Tomislav Sunic, born in Yugoslavia and teaching political science in the U.S., has warned that "Undoubtedly, the example of Yugoslavia could be used in observing similar ethnic disruptions that are likely to occur in South Africa, India, or *tomorrow's California.*"[226] (The italicization is Sunic's. His prescience may be the better appreciated if it is noted that he wrote these words at least a year prior to the Los Angeles riots of 1992.)

Another significant parallel between Yugoslavia and the U.S. is the geographic dispersal of ethnic groups in both countries. A glance at the ethnic map of Yugoslavia reveals a pattern suggestive of a patchwork quilt. There are, for example, numerous "islands" of Muslim majorities scattered across Bosnia. Dennison Rusinow, writing in *Foreign Policy,* summarizes the situation as follows:

> Serbs and Croats in diaspora across Yugoslavia are the primary reason for doubting a smooth disintegration: 24 per cent of all Serbs live outside Serbia, mostly in Bosnia-Herzegovina and Croatia; 22 per cent of all Croats live outside Croatia, mostly in Bosnia-Herzegovina and Serbia's Vojvodina. Croatia's Serb minority, 12 per cent of the Republic's population, is a majority in a number of districts, particularly around the republic's horseshoe border with Bosnia-Herzegovina. Frightful experiences in the World War II "Independent State of Croatia" still haunt minority populations there . . . .
>
> The situation is complicated by historic and ethnic claims by both Croatia and Serbia to Bosnia-Herzegovina, a complex patchwork of 1.3 million Serbs, 758,000 Croats, and 1.6 million Serbo-Croatian-speaking Muslims, . . .[227]

The tripartite ethnic division of this area has, much as in Miami, led to the development of tripartite and parallel institutions in virtually every area of life. This situation is delineated fully in Sabrina P. Ramet's aptly named *Balkan Babel: Politics, Culture and Religion in Yugoslavia.*[228] Comparing the similar situations of Miami and Bosnia-Herzegovina offers yet another illustration of the principle that behavioral assimilation (even after being enforced for decades by an authoritarian regime) is not to be confused with structural assimilation.

Yugoslavia has its own "Aztlan," the southern province of Kosovo, which borders on Albania. When Yugoslavia was founded, Kosovo had a Serbian majority. The migration of Albanians into Yugoslavia and their high birthrates led to the rise of an overwhelming Albanian majority in Kosovo. The non-Slavic, Muslim Albanians now claim Kosovo on demographic grounds and seek its annexation by Albania, while the Serbs retain a historic claim to the province.[229]

During 1992 and 1993, the civil war in Yugoslavia made that rapidly disintegrating state a focal point for American foreign policy. Less publicized, because less violent in their manifestation, were similar fissiparous ventures within the Commonwealth of Independent States which had replaced the Union of Soviet Socialist Republics. In mid-1992, for example, the Dniester Republic, with a population of 600,000, most of whom were Russians and Ukrainians, declared its independence from Moldova, most of whose population total of 4.4 million were of Rumanian origin.[230] Given the small size of the Dniester Republic, it will probably soon be absorbed by Russian-Ukrainian irredentism. Nonetheless, it serves as an example of the extremes manifested by the devolutionary impulse after decades of authoritarian centralism.

No event in Eastern Europe, however, illustrated the persistence of ethnic separatism more forcefully than the remarkable resurgence of nationalism among the Volga Germans and other *Volksdeutsche*. Against all predictions and expectations, the Volga Germans, as of 1992, seemed ready to regain self-determination while *Volksdeutsche* in other areas of Eastern Europe won recognition of their status as a distinct society within their host nations.

As recently as May 7, 1989, when the following account appeared in *The Times* of London, there appeared to be no hope for a future for the two million Volga Germans living in the Soviet Union:

. . . . the Germans have no territory to call their own. They are the Soviet Union's largest homeless and forgotten nation. Until a few months ago, the Soviet press never mentioned their existence. Their language, culture and religion are dying out.

An independent society known as Wiedergeburt (rebirth) has been set up to re-establish a German republic in their historical homeland on the Volga, but their chances of success seem slim, and a reaction has already set in among local Communist party leaders.

The Germans, who settled in Russia under Catherine the Great more than 200 years ago, were first given an autonomous republic on the Volga under Lenin in 1924. They had their own Lutheran churches, German schools, theatres and newspapers, and formed two-thirds of the republic's population.

Two months after Hitler invaded Russia in 1941, Stalin deported the Volga Germans *en masse* to the east, for ''harbouring spies and saboteurs.'' The German republic was abolished. They moved to Kazakhstan and Siberia, where as ''special settlers'' they had to register with the local commandant every week and could not move more than three miles from their villages . . . .

But the Germans remained a community apart, preserving their traditions and longing to return not to Germany, but to the Volga . . . .

In 1957, Khrushchev restored autonomous republics to all the small nations deprived of territory by Stalin, except the Germans and the Crimean Tartars, both stigmatized as collaborators with the Nazis.

In 1964, the Germans were officially rehabilitated and in 1972, they were given permission to resettle -- individually -- on the Volga. But calls for the restoration of a German republic have been consistently ignored and now it may be too late . . . . As a result, the Soviet Germans are probably heading for extinction.[231]

By the close of 1991, however, a treaty had been signed between the authorities in Moscow and the German Foreign Minister, Hans Genscher, which called for the restoration of the Volga Republic.[232] Although commonly seen as evidence of the power of Germany in Eastern Europe, this treaty is also evidence of the endurance of ethnic identity under even the most unfavorable of circumstances.

The revitalized nationalism of the *Volksdeutsche* was apparent even in the middle of Poland, in that area which was formerly the German province of Silesia. Early in 1990, "running on a campaign that stressed his identification with Germany, Henryk Kroll took 32 percent of the votes in a Senate by-election."[233] The Christian Democrats, the ruling party of reunified Germany, called in 1992 for the development of a "Euro-region" in Silesia, a region neither German nor Polish.[234]

The winning of group rights for Eastern Europe's *Volksdeutsche* has been interpreted as a diplomatic triumph by a newly reunited and powerful Germany, as if this new Germany had been anticipated by all observers all along. The reunification of Germany, however, was an unexpected manifestation of the cohesive force of German ethnicity in opposition to the contrary powers of the capitalist West and the Marxist East. According to the political ideologies of both West and East, the strength of nationalism should long ago have exhausted itself, being submerged in the triumph of a new world economic order (in the vision of the West) or a worldwide economic crisis of capitalism (in the vision of the East). The perspectives from both West and East have proven, however, to be but two contrary instances of tunnel vision, both of which have completely overlooked the reality of ethnocentrism.

The underground survival of the ethnic factor in Eastern Europe (and elsewhere) and its sudden, explosive re-emergence in separatism, irredentism, rioting, and civil war has confounded all of the classical theories of sociology. Karl Marx and Herbert Spencer were totally opposed in their assessments of capitalism, but both of them believed that the further development of capitalism and free trade would abolish the political salience of the ethnic factor. Max Weber, exponent of a value-free approach to sociology, believed that increasing bureaucratization and rationalization, in both capitalist and socialist societies, would lead to the disappearance of race, ethnicity, and language as factors in politics. Emile Durkheim believed that the advance of technology, with its increasingly complex division of labor, would lead to a submergence of the ethnic factor. (Ironically, it is France, Durkheim's native land and the most technocratic of nations, which has given rise to the world's largest racist movement, the National Front of Jean-Marie Le Pen.)

An influential group of revisionist Marxists, the Frankfurt School, the best-known among whom were Theodor Adorno, Erich Fromm, and Herbert Marcuse, recognized that sociology alone could not account for the persistence of the ethnic factor. Arguing that sociology must be supplemented with mass psychology, the Freudo-Marxists hypothesized that the patriarchal family structure characteristic of bourgeois society produces an authoritarian personality type, an extrapunitive type of person who is predisposed to ethnocentrism and the projection of imperfectly repressed hostility upon out-groups. Although they were well-known in the United States for their studies, *The Authoritarian Personality* and *One-Dimensional Man,* little has been heard from contemporary exponents of the Freudo-Marxist school since the fall of the Berlin Wall and the eruption of ethnic conflict throughout Eastern Europe. Perhaps they are reluctant to address the question of why ethnocentrism has survived in undiminished virulence in even the most proletarianized, anti-bourgeois, and anti-patriarchal of societies.

# VI

# *American Exceptionalism Has Ended*

**E** thnic conflict in Eastern Europe -- from East Germany to the Ukraine, from the Baltic to the Bosphorus -- involves peoples who differ in their dialects, languages, histories, and religions. All of these differences are cultural, not visible. They are acquired, not hereditary. Almost all of these peoples are microdiacritic in the sense in which Gordon Allport uses the term.

If there can be so much conflict among peoples who cannot recognize by sight whether particular individuals are friend or foe, then there is an even greater potential for conflict among ethnic groups which are both culturally alien and also highly visible (i.e., mesodiacritic, macrodiacritic, pandiacritic). In the Western world, it is in the United States where the greatest potential exists for confrontation between highly visible ethnic groups. It can be argued that this high visibility will act, under certain conditions, to cancel out the positive factor represented by America's tradition of liberal democracy. Americans who look to Eastern Europe and proclaim that "It can't happen here!" may be motivated by an unjustified optimism.

Erazim Kohak, a professor of sociology holding a joint appointment at Boston University and at Prague's Charles University, believes that the era of American exceptionalism has come to an end, that the U.S. is no longer exempt from being afflicted by the type of chronic inter-ethnic conflict that has re-emerged in Eastern Europe. Writing in *Daedalus*, the official journal of the American Academy of Arts and Sciences, Kohak draws the following ominous parallel between the resurgence of nationalism in Eastern Europe and ethnic tensions in America:

> . . . [A]re the dynamics of disintegration in the East that different from the strains barely concealed beneath the surface in America? Or are the loss of

personal integrity, the loss of a clear sense of reality, the loss of a legitimating vision all culturewide phenomena, not resolved in America, only masked by instant affluence financed by an ever-mounting debt? What will happen in America when the credit bubble bursts? What would happen if America decided to wipe out its debt by hyperinflating its currency, as Germany did in the 1920s? Is David Duke really that different from the nationalist demagogues who are now rehabilitating wartime quislings in the lands of the former Soviet empire?[235]

Robert J. Barro, a professor of economics at Harvard University, is less pessimistic in his prognosis for the U.S. than is Kohak, but he also sees the potential for ethnic conflict arising from competition for scarce economic goods. Barro explains the mechanism driving such conflict as follows:

Although it may be an unpleasant commentary on human nature, a central driving force in defining a state is the desire to have a reasonably homogeneous population within its borders. It is clear from observing the places where secessionist movements tend to occur, such as Yugoslavia and the Soviet Union or Spain and Canada, that ethnic identity is a central driving force. There are cases in which governments have dealt more or less successfully with sharp ethnic diversities, such as Switzerland and even the U.S., but problems are easier to pinpoint than triumphs.

Political economy explains some of the benefits from having a homogeneous population within a given state. If diversity is great -- measured say by the inequality of potential earnings -- then there is a strong incentive for people to spend their energies in efforts to redistribute income rather than to produce goods. In particular, a greater dispersion of constituent characteristics leads to the creation of interest groups that spend their time lobbying the central government to redistribute resources in their favor.[36]

The United States has, of course, dealt with ethnic diversities "more or less successfully," but in a different manner than has Switzerland. While Switzerland has accommodated ethnic diversities by political restructuring, the U.S. has, with one growing exception, limited its strategy of ethnic containment to governmental responses to demands for the redistribution of goods (by way of affirmative action and business "set-asides"). The growing exception, of course, is the policy of gerrymandering to achieve a balanced representation of ethnic groups in elected governmental bodies. In this respect, the U.S., too, has begun to follow the examples of Switzerland and Belgium. On the whole, however, the more or less successful response of the U.S. government has been limited to the production of an ever-larger pie of economic goods, in the hope that an ever-larger slice of that pie given to each contending group will prevent a public argument over whether or not it is receiving a sufficiently large slice.

Not only is avoidance of economic collapse necessary to avoid ethnic conflict, but it has become necessary for all contending parties to believe that their continued allegiance to the American polity will be rewarded with an ever-greater amount of the gross domestic product. Even a modest decline in economic production might suffice to trigger a collapse of these rising expectations. Robert J. Samuelson, an American economist, also writing at the end of 1992, sees in an ever-more successful economy the whole reason for being of the American nation. In his view, "prosperity is what binds us together; if we don't all believe in a better tomorrow, America will become a progressively less civil, less cohesive and more contentious society."[237]

According to this concept of nationhood, one based on the economic reductionism dominant from Adam Smith to T.H. Buckle, a nation is little more than a successful economy which has certain conventional geographic boundaries. Neoconservatives and revisionist Marxists, going into the new world order, agree that the nation is an almost-obsolete, almost-unnecessary division of a universally producing and consuming humanity. To affirm, to the contrary, that it is natural that "a central driving force in defining a state is the desire to have a reasonably homogeneous population within its borders" is, in many circles, tantamount to condemning oneself as an illiberal, un-democratic obscurantist.

Ethnic homogeneity is, nonetheless, as Barro notes, good political economy. Japan alone suffices to demonstrate that. Government in a multi-ethnic state must grow ever more intrusive, ever larger, and ever more costly, simply in order to preserve the political integrity of that state. This is because each ethnic bloc trusts not the representatives of another ethnic bloc, but only the state. Even then, such trust in the state is conditional, given only to a state which remains aloof from all ethnic blocs while manifesting itself to each only as a source of mollifying bounty.

The dilemma of the government in a multi-ethnic state was foreseen long before the close of the twentieth century by an observer not known for harboring illiberal sentiments. John Stuart Mill, writing in his *Considerations on Representative Government* in 1861, defined it as follows:

> Free institutions are next to impossible in a country made up of different nationalities. Among a people without fellow-feeling, especially if they read and speak different languages, the united public opinion, necessary to the working of representative government, cannot exist. The influences which form opinion and decide political acts are different in the different sections of the country . . . . The same incidents, the same acts, the same system of governments, affect them in different ways; and each fears more injury to itself from the other nationalities than from the common arbiter, the state.[238]

Mill's assessment is not obsolete, not inapplicable to the twentieth century, nor is it limited to the Anglo-Saxon world.[239] Gunnar Myrdal, a Swedish Social Democrat who is well-known in the U.S. as the author of *An American Dilemma,* looked to America again when he wrote "The Case Against Romantic Ethnicity." Even in 1974, Myrdal found it to be self-evident that ethnic divisions were undermining any social consensus in America and exacerbating existing evils. His analysis reveals the immensity of the task confronting the government of an ethnically divided state:

> Fragmentation and passivity on economic and political issues among the lower strata of the American nation are part of a much larger problem: the relatively low degree of institutional and psychological integration of its people. Associated with this is the high degree of American tolerance of corruption and also the great prevalence of crime and violence. The United States has several times as many murders and other brutal crimes, as well as softer but even more socially deranging upper-class felonies, as the northwestern European countries. This is a truly astonishing fact in a nation with so many very good and law-obeying people, a fact which raises questions of loyalty and solidarity.
>
> What is obviously needed in America is a much higher identification with the nation as a whole, not merely people identifying within their separate ethnic groups.[240]

Less than two decades after Myrdal wrote those words, it had become apparent that identification with the nation as a whole had been lessened so that individuals, through identifying with their respective ethnic groups, might maximize their influence on a government seen as a means of distribution of both publicly and privately produced goods. Increasingly, ethnic groups had been mobilized not to "higher identification with the nation as a whole," but to a contest to determine which group would control, in Mill's terms, "the common arbiter, the state." This process has been described by Joseph Rothschild in his *Ethnopolitics* as the "politicisation of ethnicity," which is "a dialectical process that preserves ethnic groups by emphasizing their singularity and yet also engineers and lubricates their modernisation by transforming them into political conflict groups for the modern political arena, where they must deploy cosmopolitan modern skills and resources."[241]

Obviously, "political conflict groups" are most readily mobilized when they are assembled from macrodiacritic or pandiacritic populations. These groupings are, in a metaphorical sense, already "pre-organized" by Nature. It is more "cost-effective" to form political groupings from the ranks of people who can immediately and literally see themselves as belonging to the group rather than from a mixed multitude whose allegiance must be won, cultivated, and continually sustained by expensive campaigns of propaganda and advertising. Just as, historically, a faith has always triumphed over a philosophy, when the allegiance of masses is in question, because of the possibility of a simplistic, symbolic transmission of the former, so, too, are political allegiances based on a visible commonalty more enduring than those based on a calculus of interests. An allegiance arising from an awareness of belonging to a visible group may be deplored as irrational or evil or narrow-minded, but it cannot be denied that it has a basis which is natural.

Gerrymandering to ensure representation of visible ethnic minorities in elected offices may lead to the empowerment of such groups, but it also, contrary to the hopes of Myrdal and others in the social democratic tradition, reinforces ethnic separatism by reducing an election to an implicit ethnic census. A successful campaign results from the mobilization of as many members of an ethnic group as possible into a "political conflict group." Richard L. Morrill refers to this phenomenon as one of the "Dilemmas of Pluralism in the United States." One example he cites illustrates the process described by Rothschild:

> Success in registering blacks resulted in dramatic increases in black political representation at all levels, but only if they remained spatially segregated. This created an extremely difficult dilemma for the black community between the benefits of group self-esteem and power through remaining separate and electing more officials, and the benefits to many individuals, and probably to the group in the longer run of pushing to integrate . . . .
>
> This formal recognition of group rights also extends, in voting and redistricting, to the American Indians and the population of Hispanic origin. Unfortunately, these precedents have led to a wider separatism, and to the general proposition that every group, for whatever purpose, deserves representation and special protection merely because of its existence.[242]

Thus, "affirmative gerrymandering," a device originally intended to contain or manage ethnic conflict, has become a means of sustaining conflict by rewarding and institutionalizing a political mobilization of "us against them." Moreover, the ongoing demographic shift, driven by immigration out of control, will increase pressures to extend "affirmative gerrymandering" to areas of the country far from the South, areas where there are burgeoning populations of Hispanics and Asians. The best outcome from all this "mappism" for which one can hope will be a political structure which resembles that of Belgium rather more than that of Bosnia.

Government in a multi-ethnic state, especially one divided among two or more highly visible population groups, in order to preserve that state, must assume a role which both conservatives and liberals can only find to be undesirable. Conservatives must find objectionable an ever-growing, ever-more-intrusive government. Liberals, while not objecting to growth in government, cannot be happy that the government, rather than advancing the public good, is called upon to deploy its energies simply to prevent a breakdown or schism within the state. That this is increasingly the role of government in the U.S. is reflected in the fact that the rhetoric of presidential campaigns has begun to center on the candidates' promises to restore a lost social consensus. After each election, however, the process of mobilization of ethnic minorities into "political conflict groups" goes on unabated.

As the United States becomes ever more pluralistic, both elected officials and the bureaucracy find themselves increasingly confronted with the dire need to search for answers to these questions: Under what conditions can the government of a multi-ethnic state be successful? What strategy can be implemented to assure political stability? What tactics can be employed to realize that strategy?

Arend Lijphart is probably the foremost authority on the governmental systems of multi-ethnic states. His *Democracy in Plural Societies,* published in 1977, examines successful governmental systems in Austria, Belgium, Switzerland, and the Netherlands. A successful system is one having "political stability," which Lijphart defines as "system maintenance, civil order, legitimacy, and effectiveness."[243] Consociational democracy, Lijphart's name for such a successful system, is defined by him as "government by a grand coalition of the political leaders of all significant segments of the plural society . . . [which features a] a mutual veto or 'concurrent' majority rule . . . proportionality [in] political representation, civil service appointments, and allocation of public funds [and] . . . a high degree of autonomy for each segment to run its own internal affairs."[244]

Lijphart's paradigm becomes more understandable when it is applied to American political history. When the United States was a young republic, the structure of its society was relatively homogeneous and its elites, to the extent that more than one elite existed, were coalescent. Hence, the early nation approached being a depoliticized democracy in which party divisions were only nascent. When, however, the elites of the North and South grew to assume an adversarial stance towards one another, with the Northern elite claiming control of the central government, a centripetal democracy arose which soon collapsed into civil war. The U.S. in the twentieth century has an increasingly pluralistic structure with uneasily coalescent elites; it is a consociational democracy.

The *sine qua non* of consociational democracy is the creation of a working coalition of the elites of the different ethnic blocs. In Lijphart's words, "The political stability of the consociational democracies must be explained in terms of an additional factor -- cooperation by the leaders of the different groups which transcends the segmented or subcultural cleavages at the mass level."[245] If elites are adversarial rather than coalescent, the democracy will be centrifugal, en route to self-destruction. Lijphart offers the following paradigm of possibilities for democracy in multi-ethnic states:

| | Structure of Society | |
| Elites | Homogeneous | Plural |
| --- | --- | --- |
| Coalescent | Depoliticized Democracy | Consociational Democracy |
| Adversarial | Centripetal Democracy | Centrifugal Democracy[246] |

Lijphart believes that elite coalescence is largely "motivated by an awareness of the dangers inherent in segmental cleavages and a desire to avert them. An . . . additional factor is the prior existence of a tradition of elite accommodation."[247] Elite coalescence in America arises from an awareness that, in the words of Seymour Martin Lipset, "Democracy needs cleavage within linguistic or religious groups, not between them."[248] Hence, governing elites agree that tolerance is America's highest civic virtue, and racism its most heinous evil. Even if there is much hypocrisy behind these professions of faith, they must be accepted without question if elite coalescence is to be maintained.

If elite coalescence fails, the elite of a minority ethnic bloc may adopt one or more of the strategies which Anthony Smith has enumerated. The majority ethnic bloc may react with attempts to maintain its political supremacy. If the contending ethnic blocs are roughly equal in numbers, the conflict for control of the state apparatus will be unending and often violent. In that case, while democracy may be maintained within the various ethnic blocs, the cohesiveness of the state as a whole will be subjected to increasing stress.

One unambiguous instance of centrifugal democracy in the Western world is in Northern Ireland, where, according to Lijphart, "The Protestants and Catholics of Northern Ireland form two quite distinct and separate segments with their own social, educational, and recreational organizations."[249] This degree of separatism, similar to that in Miami or Monterey Park, is not sufficient to split Northern Ireland in two because "Segmental isolation is only social and not geographical; although the cities have become increasingly ghettoized since 1968, the two populations are highly interspersed territorially."[250] Since the contending groups in Northern Ireland are microdiacritic, not macrodiacritic or pandiacritic as they are in the U.S., the development of geographic separatism is a much slower process.

George Schoepflin, writing in 1991 in the *Journal of International Affairs*, assesses the feasibility of consociational democracy in the states of central and

eastern Europe and, inadvertently, provides some insights into how it functions in the United States. He defines consociationalism as the effort ''to draw
all the different segments into the decision-making process through elite
representation, a kind of grand coalition.'' It operates upon the basis of a kind
of unwritten constitution or gentlemen's agreement, which recognizes that
''the government should keep much of its negotiation behind closed doors in
order to prevent popular mobilization around a particular issue that could be
related to group identity; and a set of tacit rules of the game . . . .''[251]

How viable is consociationalism as a strategy for political stability? Schoepflin believes that

> [I]t requires two essential conditions to succeed. In the first place, all the groups
> concerned must be willing to work toward accommodation and be ready to
> bargain; that, in turn, implies the creative use of both substantive and pro-
> cedural solutions that will help all parties . . . . all groups must work to avoid
> zero-sum-game situations, . . . ; above all, there must be no major winners or
> losers. Second, the leaders of a group must be able to secure the support of their
> followers. The success of this will depend on the confidence of the members of
> the group in the system as a whole -- a recognition that their interests will be
> taken into consideration in the bargaining. Otherwise, the consociational bar-
> gains will fall apart. Thus, the leadership of the group must be able to sell
> solutions to the membership. Society, as well as leadership, must be sophisti-
> cated for consociational solutions to work well.[252]

Whatever may be the long-term prospects for consociational democracy in
small, affluent Western European nations, they would seem to be dim in the
United States, where almost irreversible demographic and economic trends
militate against its two essential conditions. If the U.S. grows to 392 million
people by 2050, as has been projected by the U.S. Census Bureau, without
having solved the seemingly unsolvable problems arising from a scarcity of
vital natural resources (such as arable land, fossil fuels, and clean water), how
can a competition for scarce economic goods be seen as other than a zero-sum-
game? When ''the leaders'' (i.e., the elites of each ethnic bloc) fail to deliver
the economic goods which their followers need and desire, how will they ''be
able to secure the support of their followers''?

Experts may disagree as to when shortages of economic goods will become
acute, but all agree that the supply of the resources essential to their production
is definitely limited. David Pimentel, professor of agriculture at Cornell
University, examines the great triad of resources in his ''Land, Energy, and
Water: The Constraints Governing Ideal Population Size,'' published in 1992.
According to Pimentel, ''Nearly all the arable land is in production and in fact
some marginal land is also in production.''[253] Pimentel concludes that the
living standards of 1992 can be sustained through the replacement of fossil

fuels by solar energy only if the population of the U.S. were to be somehow reduced to 100 million.[254] The limits of the water supply are also becoming evident in the 1990s. "Currently, groundwater overdraft is 25 percent greater than its replenishment rate, with the result that our mammoth groundwater aquifers are being mined at an alarming rate."[255]

It is commonly believed that a technological breakthrough (e.g., "cold" fusion and/or "room-temperature" superconductivity) may develop energy sources other than fossil fuels, energy sources which can be applied to the recovery of arable land and the purification of water. Ironically, however, population pressures, the very condition making urgent the need to find substitutes for fossil fuels, may prevent the realization of a technological breakthrough. It is likely that the immediate demands of a larger population will take priority over the needs of researchers when appropriations bills are being considered.

Population pressures translated into political pressures are even more likely to prevent the widespread implementation of those alternative and sustainable technologies which already exist. This is the warning which Paul J. Werbos sounded in 1992 in his "Energy and Population: Transitional Issues and Eventual Limits." Werbos, program director of the National Science Foundation after a decade of service with the Department of Energy, concludes that "the growth of population and the composition of this growth in the next two to three decades is possibly the most serious problem reducing our chance of a successful transition to sustainable technology. At first glance, the connection may not be obvious, but it is really quite strong."[256]

Although a surplus of labor may benefit employers, it will worsen the nation's social problems. Vernon M. Briggs, Jr., professor of human resource economics at Cornell University, argues in his "Political Confrontation with Economic Reality: Mass Immigration in the Post-Industrial Age," published in 1992, that the surplus of labor resulting from the renewal of mass immigration represents the wrong kind of human resources. Since the American economy continues to shift away from goods-producing industries, which have traditionally required a low level of skills, to service industries, requiring higher levels of skills, "the current pattern of mass immigration of primarily unskilled people is a direct threat to the nation's well-being."[257] This mass of unskilled labor is a particular threat to the nation's underclass. There is a shortage of skilled workers among the underclass, but an influx of cheap alien labor will militate against efforts to develop their skills. As Briggs explains,

> If mass and unguided immigration continues, it is unlikely that there will be sufficient pressure to enact the long-term human resource development policies needed to prepare and to incorporate these groups into the mainstream economy. Instead, it is likely that the heavy but unplanned influx of immigrant labor

will serve, by providing both competition and alternatives, to maintain the social marginalization of many citizen Blacks and citizen Hispanics. As a result, the chance to eliminate once and for all the underclass in the U.S. economy will be lost -- probably forever.[258]

Writing in 1985 "On the Political Consequences of Scarcity and Economic Decline," Ted Robert Gurr, professor of international studies at the University of Colorado, presents an overview of the extensive literature on this topic and corrects widespread misconceptions. Gurr finds that both "ecological pessimists" and "technological optimists" offer political prescriptions which "rest on unexamined premises about the malleability of political values and institutions."[259] Gurr cites William Ophuls' *Ecology and the Politics of Scarcity* (1977) and Harold Stretton's *Capitalism, Socialism and the Environment* (1975) as exemplars of these two schools of thought, yet finds that they agree "that the onset of scarcity in prosperous societies leads to an intensification of conflict." Gurr sees particular merit in Robert Heilbroner's argument, in his *An Inquiry into the Human Prospect* (1974), that there are "limits . . . to the adaptability of political structures."[260]

Gurr believes that the economic and political consequences of scarcity depend on its magnitude and the rapidity of its onset:

> Duration is crucial; so long as decline is seen as temporary, advantaged groups are likely to accept policies of relief and redistribution as the price of order and the resumption of growth. Once it is accepted as a persisting condition, however, they will increasingly exert economic and political power to regain their absolute and relative advantages. Similarly, the gradual onset of scarcity-induced decline, rather than an abrupt crisis seems more conducive to increased inequalities because advantaged groups thus have more time to mobilize resources in defense of their advantages . . . . the psychology and politics of economic crises thought to be temporary can be expected to differ significantly from the crises that occur when societies encounter intractable ecological limits.[261]

Although he makes no reference to consociational democracy, Gurr employs concepts which parallel those of Lijphart and Schoepflin when he considers how scarcity affects the political process. Noting that political stability and democracy depend on an expanding economy, he describes as follows the political consequences of long-term economic decline:

> The advent of economic stasis changes the politics of distribution from one of optimistic cooperation (a non-zero-sum game in which cooperation is expected to lead to positive payoffs for all parties) to one of antagonistic cooperation (a game in which cooperation, or compliance, is required to avoid negative

payoffs for all parties). In the short term, optimistic attitudes may prevail. In the longer-run more and more claimants will conclude that economic stasis is an enduring condition. One rational inference is that the prospects of any collectivity -- organized workers, an employers' federation, an ethnic minority -- for economic gain depends on inducing or coercing others to settle for less . . . . the new political issue is how to distribute privation. In this negative-sum-game situation there is every reason to think that group conflict over distribution will intensify.[262]

Under such conditions, conflict resolution becomes impossible. Conflict management becomes a highly desired goal of the governing elites, but conflict containment emerges as the best reality for which they can hope. Gurr notes that protest is the favored tactic of a collectivity seeking redistribution in its favor when the economy is expanding. Under such circumstances, governing elites can afford to mollify those who protest. When goods to be distributed do not exist; i.e., according to Gurr, "Under conditions of persisting and unregulated decline, . . . one would expect an erosion of the beliefs and policies which sustain limited forms of collective action, and the reemergence of popular attitudes favoring more radical and violent forms of action."[263]

Gurr believes that the United Kingdom, among all advanced industrial societies, is closest to facing this condition of economic stasis. Ecological factors figure in the decline because "Britain has lost the resource and locational advantages it enjoyed at the onset of the industrial revolution and has not developed compensatory technological advantages."[264] Gurr cites the evidences of Britain's economic stagnation. To these might be added the resurgence, in 1993, of a serious challenge to British unity in the form of Scottish nationalism.[265]

Gurr does not attempt to place the United States in relation to the concepts of stasis or decline, but his survey of growth-regenerating policies and of strategies for adapting to ecological constraints is definitely apropos. The former, even if successful, can only contain inter-group conflicts at best, while the latter, even while being implemented, will definitely tell everyone living in the U.S. that the era of rising expectations has become part of history.

The effectiveness of growth-regenerating policies (e.g., "stimulation of investment, promotion of technological innovation, and in the face of resource scarcity, development of new domestic and alternative foreign sources of supply") depends on ecological limits as well as political factors.[266] When such policies are reshaped to meet the challenge of ecological constraints, they can evolve into a limited strategy or a comprehensive strategy. Limited strategies "focus on redistributing the costs of scarcity," while comprehensive strategies are "those based on the assumption that resource scarcity is an enduring constraint and designed to respond to that condition by reducing total demand."[267]

Ecological forecasting has suffered from an incursion of individuals, some of them Luddites, who resort to exaggerations replete with references to "collapse," "catastrophe," and "entropy." Such excesses by those who might be called "environmental publicists" have led many otherwise well-informed Americans to dismiss all considerations of environmental problems. It is fortunate, therefore, that in 1993 the first report was published by the project on Environmental Change and Acute Conflict, which is jointly sponsored by the University of Toronto and the American Academy of Arts and Sciences. Although the project is an interdisciplinary effort, it has a firm base in the natural sciences. The following excerpts from the project's report on "Environmental Change and Violent Conflict," published in *Scientific American,* confirm the conclusions of Gurr and others:

> . . . . [t]he environment is but one variable in a series of political, economic and social factors that can bring about turmoil. Indeed, some skeptics claim that scarcities of renewable resources are merely a minor variable that sometimes links existing political and economic factors to subsequent social conflict.
>
> The evidence we have assembled supports a different view. Such scarcity can be an important force behind changes in the politics and economics governing resource use. It can cause powerful actors to strengthen, in their favor, an inequitable distribution of resources . . . .
>
> Skeptics often use a different argument. They state that conflict arising from resource scarcity is not particularly interesting, because it has been common throughout human history. We maintain, though, that renewable resource scarcities of the next 50 years will probably occur with a speed, complexity and magnitude unprecedented in history. Entire countries can now be deforested in a few decades, most of a region's topsoil can disappear in a generation, and acute ozone depletion may take place in as few as 20 years . . . .[268]

It is highly probable, given trends evident in the 1990s, that at some point in the first half of the twenty-first century, downward pressures on living standards, largely arising from scarcities of resources, will combine with population pressures and a fundamental shift in the ethnic origins of the U.S. population to produce a protracted crisis unprecedented in American history. The latter element in the crisis -- the shift in ethnic origins -- which will be tantamount to a transformation of the United States from a First World nation into an unstable mix of First World and Third World peoples, will produce a political crisis of such dimensions as to be insoluble within the traditional limits of American governance.

By 2050, according to 1993 projections published by the U.S. Census Bureau, the percentages of major ethnic groups in the U.S. population will be as follows: whites, 50%; Hispanics, 23%; blacks, 16%; Asians, 10%; American Indians, 1%. These projections, which belatedly corroborated Leon

Bouvier's work, are based on an annual net influx of 880,000 immigrants, a total almost certainly lower than the combined legal flow of around 900,000 per year allowed by the Immigration Act of 1990 and illegal immigration of 300,000 to 500,000 per year.[269]

The baleful meaning of these projections for the survival of democracy in the United States is simply this: Given a continuation of long-established patterns of immigration and birth rates, there will be in the U.S., sometime around 2050 if not sooner, a point at which the country will no longer have a single majority ethnic bloc. At best, it will have a large ethnic bloc of European Americans who will constitute only a plurality and who will find themselves confronted with only slightly smaller minority ethnic blocs.

The disappearance of a core ethnic bloc in the United States will undermine whatever degree of consociational democracy yet exists. This is because consociational democracy in the U.S. has always been dependent on a fortuitous situation in which the white or European American majority is led by an elite which retains the confidence of its co-ethnic followers as well as the provisional trust of the elites of the other ethnic blocs. This situation is the coalescence or coalition of elites upon which consociationalism depends.

The masses of European Americans have accepted an elite which attempts to represent itself as being the elite of the entire nation, not simply the elite of one ethnic bloc. This fiction of altruistic liberalism on the part of the European American leadership has been accepted by its followers largely because the latter, being clearly in the majority, have had the psychological reassurance that "this is our country." When, however, the European American majority finds itself threatened with becoming a minority and has indeed already become a minority in large regions of the country, the coalition of elites will be destabilized by a crisis of confidence among its European American followers.

Throughout the latter half of the twentieth century, the European American elite has led its rank and file to think of inter-ethnic relations in terms of prejudiced individuals among the majority and victimized individuals among the minorities. The paradigm of corporate pluralism, which sees inter-ethnic relations in terms of group dynamics, has been resisted, largely because it is contrary to the Anglo-Saxon legal tradition, which stresses individual accountability. During the 1990s, however, the paradigm of group dynamics, which stresses the responsibilities, rights, and entitlements of groups, has gained an almost unassailable role in public policy and has begun to loom larger than the paradigm of prejudiced/victimized individuals. The unresolved conflict of these two paradigms, one in the ascendant and one in decline, explains the apparent paradox that a minority may organize overtly ethnic political conflict groups, which are accepted as the justified support groups of the victimized, while any similar organization on behalf of members of the majority is denounced by the European American elite as racist.

The rank and file of European Americans, beginning to see themselves as members of but one contending group among others, and seeing that other groups have leaders who are explicitly ethnic leaders, will feel threatened if they continue to lack such leaders. The politically stabilizing fiction that European American leaders are not themselves ethnic leaders, but are leaders of "all Americans, regardless of race, color, or creed," will then face a challenge from a side other than that of the ethnic minorities. The established European American elite, well aware that its pose of altruistic liberalism has been viewed with skepticism by non-European elites, will be exceedingly reluctant to placate their restive rank and file at the risk of threatening the coalescence of elites.

Rank and file European Americans, seeking leadership as militant on behalf of their interests as is the leadership of a minority ethnic bloc, will begin to transfer their allegiance to a new leadership, a rising counter-elite of those whom Erazim Kohak calls "nationalist demagogues." The result will be a collapse of consociational democracy even before a complete revolution of elites has taken place. When, in other words, European Americans begin to think of themselves as such and demand ethnically conscious European American leaders, then America will have become America Balkanized, a nation without Americans, just as Yugoslavia, in the early 1990s, became a nation without Yugoslavs; i.e., no longer a viable nation.

Those who think that this scenario is wildly improbable might do well to recall the situation which developed in 1991, when it seemed possible that a man generally considered to be a racist demagogue would be elected to the governorship of a Southern state. Alarm was widespread among U.S. governing circles. An unprecedented political mobilization took place which enlisted the support of persons rarely or never associated with electoral politics. Political figures from the President on down endorsed the demagogue's opponent even though he represented an opposing political party. Leaders in industry, finance, and commerce, clergymen of all denominations, educators, entertainers and celebrities, and labor leaders all spoke out against the demagogue's candidacy. All newspapers save one small rural weekly endorsed the demagogue's opponent. Serious plans were announced to subject the state to an economic boycott should the demagogue be elected.

Despite this alignment of forces against him, the demagogue won a majority of the European American voters of the state. Only an overwhelming non-European American vote in favor of the demagogue's opponent prevented his election. An almost audible sigh of relief arose from the ranks of governing circles, where the fear was widespread that the election of even one such demagogue would begin a decline in the credibility of the European American elite. Certainly the election of even one such demagogue would suffice to endanger the policy of discussing sensitive issues only behind closed doors. Consociational democracy in America, even in the 1990s, is a perilous balancing act which might be overturned by even a few irresponsible outsiders. The descent to Avernus is easy.

Despite the increasing evidences of strain within America's consociational democracy, it is still assumed by many that these are simply unfortunate episodes. It remains tempting to believe that America represents a great exception in world history, that the United States began with a blank slate, that the new nation left behind all of the old quarrels of Europe. In the words of Goethe, "America, you have it better than our old continent." From this perspective, the prospect of America Balkanized seems fanciful. Despite an overwhelming influx of immigrants during the nineteenth century, according to this argument, the United States government survived and became stronger than ever. Sooner or later, millions of Irish, British, Germans, Scandinavians and other immigrants were absorbed into the mainstream of American life and accepted a philosophy of government which was wholly new to them. Even during the difficult transition period, in this reading of history, no great conflicts arose.

This interpretation of the role of ethnicity in American political history is, however, far removed from the facts. Not only were there marked differences in degrees of political assimilation among various immigrant groups during the nineteenth century, there is evidence that these differences have persisted even until the latter decades of the twentieth century. There is demonstrable evidence of continuing differences in the areas of political values and political participation. This evidence that differences imported from the "old countries" of Europe have been an important factor in American political history is a direct challenge to the facile assumption of American exceptionalism.

Surviving differences in political values among various American ethnic groups were given a provocative examination in "Serfdom's Legacy: An Ethnic Continuum," published by Carmi Schooler of the National Institute of Mental Health in 1976 in the *American Journal of Sociology*.[270] The abstract to Schooler's article sums up its wide-ranging thesis:

> The effects of ethnicity appear to occur along a historically determined continuum which reflects the social, legal, economic, and occupational conditions of the European countries from which American ethnic groups emigrated. Ethnic groups with a recent history of serfdom show the pragmatic legalistic morality previously found characteristic of American men working under occupational conditions limiting the individual's opportunity for self-direction. Although it is impossible to confirm each link in the causal chain, a model emphasizing the effects on ethnic groups' culture of historical conditions restricting the individual's autonomy seems a probable and parsimonious explanation of contemporary ethnic differences.[271]

According to Schooler, the major ethnic groups in America deriving from Europe can be ranked along a continuum which reflects the relative recency of the emancipation from serfdom of the peasantry in their countries of origin.[272] The continuum begins with Scandinavia, where serfdom was never established,[273] and proceeds to a midpoint with England, where serfdom was abolished during the period 1603-1625. "Because of the hypothesized importance of a tradition of autonomy and personal responsibility, Ireland, which had been a dependency under the tight control of England, is given a place in the continuum directly below England."[274] The German states, where serfdom was abolished in the period 1807-1833, occupy a place just below the midpoint of the continuum, followed by southern and central Italy, where serfdom was abolished in 1848 as part of the abolition of serfdom in the Austro-Hungarian Empire, and eastern Europe (Russia and Poland), where serfdom was abolished in 1861 by the ukase of Alexander II.[275]

Schooler sustains his hypothesis -- "that the differences found among European ethnic groups in present-day America result from cultural values which are the residue of historical processes" -- with the results of interviews of 3,101 men conducted by the National Opinion Research Center in 1964.[276] The sample excluded Jews and was limited to whites who either were born in Europe or who had a parent or grandparent born there. The interviews considered seven variables; two related to intellectual functioning ("intellectual flexibility," "intellectually demanding use of leisure time"), two related to attitudes toward authority ("authoritarian conservatism," "self-direction"), and three related to moral autonomy ("personally responsible morality," "attribution of responsibility to self for control over one's own fate," "self-deprecation, the self-critical part of self-esteem").[277]

The bulk of Schooler's analysis demonstrates how results obtained confirm his hypothesis even when one accounts for the variables of age, father's education, rurality, and region.[278] He concludes also that "ethnicity does have an effect distinct from that of adult social class."[279] Generally, individuals from ethnic groups having a longer history of freedom from serfdom showed higher levels of intellectual functioning and self-directed, rather than conforming, systems of values.[280] Schooler's conclusion is particularly noteworthy:

> Belonging to an ethnic group with a long history of freedom from serfdom has the same general empirical relationship with intellectual functioning, attitude toward authority, and moral autonomy as does working in a substantively complex or self-directed job. Both conditions seem to produce persons who are intellectually more effective, who believe that they have some control over their lives, and who feel that the ultimate locus of ethical responsibility is within themselves, rather than in authorities, the law, or other external enforcers of conformity. The internalization of ethical responsibility of those

from such ethnic groups also seems to limit their ability to shift the burden of their ethical responsibility onto others, thus tending to make them more self-critical.[281]

Of the seven variables Schooler considered, at least two, those concerning attitudes toward authority, are obviously political values. "Authoritarian conservatism" is not necessarily acceptance of a "rightist" ideology; rather, it is a stolid, unthinking acceptance of whatever values are established by those who rule any society. Similarly, a low sense of "self-direction" also renders an individual more amenable to unquestioning acceptance of authority. "Intellectual flexibility" and "intellectually demanding use of leisure time," which seem to be apolitical variables, are, in fact, the basic virtues of an informed citizen. The three factors coalescing in a sense of internalized "moral autonomy" are essential to the preservation of law and order in the absence of a high degree of governmental regulation and intervention. Obviously, a people not long removed from serfdom will both accept and need the rule of a strong, authoritarian state, while the obverse will be true of a people having in its ranks a large independent yeomanry.

It may be supposed, however, that Schooler's thesis, even if otherwise validated, would prove to have little practical value in understanding the contemporary United States simply because it is limited to the always nebulous realm of values and attitudes rather than measurable behavior. However, at least one researcher, Andrew Greeley of the National Opinion Research Center, has studied one important area of behavior -- political participation -- and has concluded that ethnicity is "a meaningful predictor" of such behavior. Greeley's "Political Participation Among Ethnic Groups in the United States: A Preliminary Reconnaissance," published in a 1974 issue of the *American Journal of Sociology*,[282] presents in its results, independently of Schooler, an ethnic continuum analogous to his. Greeley found significant differences in levels of political participation among major "religioethnic groups" in the U.S. even "when social class is held constant.'"[283] Moreover, "the diversity among such collectivities is of similar magnitude to the diversity found in various nations in cross-national studies.'"[284]

Working with a "weighted sample" of 3,095 Americans, Greeley considered the relationship of six predictor variables (religion, income, education, ethnicity, region, occupation) to four political participation variables (voting, campaigning, civic activity, particularized contact). He discovered that as a predictor ethnicity is "stronger than religion, region, and occupation for all four of the variables, equal to or stronger than income on two variables (voting and contact). It is the strongest predictor of both voting . . . and particularized contact, and in third place on both campaigning and civic activity.'"[285]

Making no allowance for the effects of social class and region, and combining all four political participation variables, Greeley found that on this "overall political participation scale," Irish Catholics scored 41 units; Scandinavian Protestants, 32; Jews, 19; and Polish Catholics, German Catholics, German Protestants, and Anglo-Saxon Protestants slightly more than 10."[286] Allowing for social class and for regional factors (e.g., lower levels of political participation in the South) produced the following scale of "overall political participation": Irish Catholics, 30.2; Scandinavians, 22.9; Anglo-Saxon Protestants, 7.5; German Protestants, 5.7; German Catholics, 4.5; Polish Catholics, 2.5; Irish Protestants, 0.7; Italian Catholics, -3.7; Jews, -9.9.[287]

With the exception of unusually depressed standings for the Irish Protestants and, perhaps, the Italians, Greeley's scale holding social class and region constant parallels Schooler's ethnic continuum. Greeley explains that the Jewish score is low only because of the correction for that group's social class.[288] He suggests also that the low score of the Irish Protestants is due to their location almost exclusively in the South.[289] Correcting for the low level of political participation in the South slightly elevates the Anglo-Saxons' score, but results in a drop in overall scores for German Americans, among others, who are revealed to be, in Greeley's terms, "hypopolitical," while Irish Catholics and Scandinavians retain their standings as "hyperpolitical" ethnic groups.

The ethnic continua independently discovered by Schooler and Greeley reflect different variables, but they are almost perfectly congruent. Schooler's and Greeley's findings help one to understand ethnic politics in the U.S., particularly the political histories of the Irish, Scandinavians, and Germans.

The Irish and the Scandinavians, both inclined to challenge authority (according to Schooler), and more politically active than other ethnic groups (according to Greeley), have histories of producing activists and reformers. Although most Americans think of John F. Kennedy as the representative Irish-American politician, during much of the nation's history more typical figures were charismatic reformers and demagogues, such as Denis Kearney, Ignatius Donnelly, Father Charles E. Coughlin, Joseph R. McCarthy, and Eugene McCarthy. After 1900, the Scandinavians showed a radical propensity by becoming active in agrarian, third-party movements, notably the Non-Partisan League and the Farmer-Labor party. Notable figures include Charles Lindbergh, Sr., and Floyd Olson. The Volstead Act, which put prohibition into effect in 1920, was named for Andrew Volstead, a Norwegian congressman from Minnesota.[290]

While the German Americans have produced two Presidents, Herbert Hoover and Dwight D. Eisenhower, they differed from the mass of German Americans not only in their having antecedents from the early immigration of the colonial period, but in coming from long lines of religious dissenters,

Quakers and Mennonites respectively. In strong contrast to the Irish and the Scandinavian records of taking the initiative and seeking innovative reforms, the record of German-American politics has been one of mere reaction to the initiatives of other groups, when it has not been a simple accommodation to them.

The relatively low levels of political participation among German Americans as well as their greater willingness to accept authority may, ironically, have contributed to political stability in the U.S. For whatever reasons, German Americans did not mount significant opposition either to the legal suppression of the use of German as a language of instruction in the public schools or to the entrance of the U.S. into two European wars against the German homeland. Thomas J. Archdeacon, in his *Becoming American: An Ethnic History,* suggests, in the following, the fateful significance of this German-American acquiescence:

> . . . the blatantly repressive actions taken during World War I against the propagation of German culture in the United States . . . . did not directly inculcate an American culture. They did, however, undermine the only European group that had ever enjoyed the numerical strength, prosperity, high racial status, and ties to a powerful homeland needed to sustain in the United States a culture competitive with the British.[291]

The evidence of history and the researches of Schooler and Greeley suggest that German Americans acquiesced to "Anglo-conformity," rather than being assimilated to it. Their acceptance of the Anglo-American political tradition which begins with the U.S. Constitution and goes back to William Blackstone, John Locke, Magna Charta, and the Anglo-Saxon common law probably owed more to a Continental tradition of obeisance to authority than to any conscious experience of conversion.

While "Anglo-conformity" seemed to work as a style of cultural assimilation as far as the German Americans were concerned, the fear was widespread among Americans of the old stock that it would not be accepted by other groups of immigrants. The old Americans reacted to each new wave of immigration with a counter-wave of nativism. Three great periods of ethnic conflict and reaction led millions to join or support nativist organizations such as the American Party in the 1850s, the American Protective Association in the 1890s, and the Ku Klux Klan in the 1920s.[292] Far from being the product of ruling class machinations aimed at dividing the working class, these nativist movements enrolled millions of working-class people and were actively combatted by the elite. Nativist mass movements came to an end only when mass immigration subsided due to restrictive legislation passed in the 1920s, and virtually ceased during the Great Depression of the 1930s, and the Second

World War.

According to the popular interpretation based on the theory of American exceptionalism, ethnic conflict arose in nineteenth century America only because immigrant groups were isolated from the mainstream of society. This isolation led to the development among the old stock Americans of deeply ingrained prejudices against the later arrivals. The assimilation of the latter into the social mainstream led to an overcoming of the prejudicial misconceptions held by Americans of the old stock. This interpretation is, of course, rooted in American exceptionalism, which denies the relevance for America of the history of Europe, where ethnic conflicts have reached their greatest intensity precisely where there has been a minimal amount of isolation of the various ethnic groups. Only in America has it been presumed that a maximum amount of interaction among groups will lead to an optimum level of mutual understanding.

At least one painstakingly researched historical study contradicts this exceptionalist theory. Susan Olzak, professor of sociology at Cornell University, published in 1992 her book-length study of ethnic conflict in America during the period 1877-1914, *The Dynamics of Ethnic Competition and Conflict*. Olzak studied "instances of ethnic collective action" in 77 cities, using "event-history methods of analysis to explore models of racial and ethnic confrontations, riots, violence, protest marches, and other forms of public and collective activity organized around racial and ethnic boundaries."[293]

Olzak applied ecological theory to group relations to conclude that ethnic groups which have found in occupational specialization a kind of "ecological niche" may be less exposed than others to conflict-generating competition. She examines both economic and political competition, including the publication of ethnically-oriented and/or foreign-language newspapers as a kind of ethnic collective action, and concludes that "competition intensifies the salience of ethnic boundaries and promotes spontaneous forms of ethnic collective action . . . . ethnic conflict surges when barriers to ethnic group contact and competition begin to break down."[294] Olzak reaches a conclusion, which she summarizes as follows, that directly contradicts the popular theory regarding the cause of ethnic conflict:

> Earlier theories of ethnic collective action emphasized the importance of ethnic/racial segregation and repression for understanding the persistence of ethnic boundaries and ethnic politics. This book suggests a more complicated relationship between segregation and conflict. While extreme levels of ethnic segregation in occupations may reinforce ethnic solidarity, it does not appear to foster ethnic conflict. Rather, extreme levels of segregation are best analyzed as outcomes of competition. According to this view, extreme segregation reduces levels of contact and competition, thus lowering the rate of conflict among

groups. Instead, ethnic desegregation tends to produce conflicts that generate attempts at repression and resegregation.[295]

The most parsimonious explanation may be that the decline of ethnic separatism is coeval with the mobilization of ethnic groups as political conflict groups. According to this interpretation, the various forms of ethnic separatism described by Anthony Smith may be a strategy of *reculer pour mieux sauter*. It is noteworthy that Olzak believes that the patterns of group conflict she has described are as present in the contemporary United States as they were in the late nineteenth century.

Even the most friendly of European observers have not claimed for America an exemption from all conflict in the future. For them, American exceptionalism was only a temporary exemption from the class conflict plaguing Europe, a frontier period which would last only as long as the new nation did not feel the pressures of population. G.W.F. Hegel, although he called America "the land of the future," predicted that "North America will be comparable with Europe . . . . after the immeasurable space which that country presents to its inhabitants shall have been occupied, and the members of the political body shall have begun to be pressed back on each other." [296] T.H. Huxley, speaking at the founding of the Johns Hopkins University in 1876, predicted that in 1976, the United States would have a population of 200 million, and that "as population thickens in your great cities, and the pressure of want is felt, the gaunt spectre of pauperism will stalk among you, and communism and socialism will claim to be heard." [297]

If American exceptionalism ever existed in any form, it existed only as long as the frontier was open, a period of development which ended no later than 1890. Even the period of the open frontier was not without its conflicts, as noted. Going into the twenty-first century, the United States is far away from the frontier experience. Already, Third World squalor grows in areas of the Southwest along with a population of homeless "street people," not to be found in Europe, in all major cities of all regions. Soon, in historical terms, 400 million people, only nominally Americans, will be locked in an escalating and unending political struggle aimed at determining who is to receive what from a dwindling supply of economic necessities.

If there was conflict in earlier decades among European American ethnic groups, all of them microdiacritic, all living in a land of seemingly boundless possibilities, is it reasonable to believe that there will be less conflict among the burgeoning populations from Third World nations, all macrodiacritic or pandiacritic, all contending for room to live within a land increasingly constrained by its ecological limits? What political legacy will these Third World immigrants bring to America? Will that political heritage be any more amenable to absorption in an ecologically overburdened America than was the legacy of Old World serfdom in a growing frontier society?

Even a cursory survey of political conditions in the Third World suggests that the prognosis cannot be one favorable to America. Asia has an enduring heritage of not simply feudalism, but of that *Oriental Despotism,* masterfully analyzed in Karl Wittfogel's thus named book, which has shown a capacity to overwhelm liberalizing Western tendencies.[298] Japan, supposedly a parliamentary democracy, has given evidence -- not limited to the controversial statements of Prime Minister Nakasone -- of being one of the most ethnocentric nations in the world.[299] China remains a one-party state. The parliamentary democracy of India may not survive an internecine warfare among the subcontinent's linguistic and religious power blocs. The future of democracy in the Philippines is very uncertain. The recent massacres in Cambodia have only ideologically motivated apologists to distinguish them from the depredations of Tamerlane. Latin America, at least from the Rio Grande to the Rio de la Plata, is a congeries of military dictatorships in which *el caudillo* follows *el golpe de estado,* and vice versa, in a succession without end. The one notable exception to this pattern, Costa Rica, is really a European colony, and may not endure much longer. Democracy is, if anything, in even more disarray in Africa. The one nation having a history of democratic forms, Liberia, fell to a military dictatorship in 1980.

Only a shortsighted ethnocentrism can account for the fond belief of many Americans that their political heritage, -- imperfectly received in the past by immigrants from nations having cultures closely related to that of the nation's founders -- will in the future transform and overwhelm all that is alien. Such a universal constant, which that all-assimilating heritage would have to be, can exist in natural history, but is not to be found in the annals of political history.

# VII
## What is a Nation?

A mericans have difficulty in understanding what a nation is because they usually equate the concepts *nation* and *state*. A nation, however, has substance while a state is merely formal. A nation is more viable than a state because it approaches being an organic entity while a state is merely a fiction generally agreed upon and written down on legal paper. Thus, one man (e.g., Washington, Mazzini, Bismarck, Masaryk) can be said to have created a state, but never a nation. A nation can exist prior to and independently of the state apparatus which represents and governs it. Examples abound of this fact, which seems to be paradoxical to many Americans, for whom the United States is merely a state; that is, a government superimposed upon an expanse of geography which is not inhabited by any particular ethnic group, a government which came into being on July 4, 1776.

One need only consider the examples of the Polish, Croatian, Slovenian, Ukrainian, Basque, Kurdish, Jewish, and Romany (Gypsy) peoples to see that, nonetheless, a nation can endure for centuries without having its name on the map. A nation can also exist far beyond the boundaries of any state that claims to speak for it. A striking example of this fact is the existence of a large portion of the German nation outside the boundaries of Germany proper. *Volksdeutsche* living anywhere in Europe may return to Germany proper, Germany as a state, and assume full citizenship even if their ancestors had left the fatherland several generations ago.

Similarly, a state, such as the Union of Soviet Socialist Republics, can exist with no acknowledged nation behind it, but only for a limited time. In the case of the USSR, internal stresses led to its devolution into its constituent nations less than a century after its creation. The distinguished Russian mathematician, Igor Shafarevich, has epitomized in the very title of his book, *Rus-*

*sophobia,* the unnatural suppression of national identity which led to the demise of the USSR. Such has been the fate of all other multi-national states, which have in the past usually called themselves empires, and which have always been more or less veiled attempts of one nation to dominate others.

A nation, then, is something other than a state, something more than a governmental apparatus. A nation endures because of an enduring ethnic core, can endure even in dispersion, even in the absence of a government. (Conversely, it can be argued that the mere creation of a governmental apparatus can never suffice to create an enduring nation.) The Greek word for nation, *ethnos,* which appears throughout the New Testament and is translated as nation, indicates the nature of this vital core of a nation. The word nation was adopted into English from the Latin *nationem,* which is defined in the *Oxford English Dictionary* (2nd ed., 1989) as "breed, stock, race, nation." *Nationem,* in turn, is derived from the Latin *nasci,* "to be born."

It is often assumed that the United States, like the USSR, had founders who established a multi-national state on the basis of a universalist ideology. In the words of Nathan Glazer, "The United States is unique among the great nations of the world in the degree to which it refuses to define itself in ethnic or religious or national terms, as our basic founding documents make clear."[300] This universalism seems to be implicit in the founding documents of the new republic, but it is debatable to what extent the Founding Fathers were truly adherents of any universalist ideology. Since any ideology is designed to justify the position of power held by a ruling elite, it is a practical necessity for a revolutionary elite to represent itself as firmly grounded in universal principles representing the aspirations of all of humanity, aspirations which were denied by the old regime. The process of rationalization involved is so automatic, so unpremeditated, that it has little of hypocrisy about it.

The French revolutionaries actually had a greater need for a universalist ideology than did the Americans because the French revolution was more sweeping in scope than the American. Both groups of eighteenth century republican revolutionaries, regardless of their other differences, shared a concept of "humanity" that was implicitly based upon their images of the educated European. The latter provided the model for their ideal of a world citizen. This seeming contradiction, again, does not reveal any conscious hypocrisy, but only the perennial ability of ideologues to sustain contradictions in their structures of thought. For this reason, the pronounced racism of many leading Enlightenment thinkers was not seen by them as a denial of their concept of humanity. Hume, Kant, and Voltaire, who epitomized the Enlightenment in their respective countries of Britain, Germany, and France, all believed that high culture is almost wholly the creation of European whites.[301]

Benjamin Franklin, the great representative of the Enlightenment in America, was no less a racist than were Hume, Kant, and Voltaire. Franklin wished to allow only "whites" to enter the new nation and argued for the exclusion of the "swarthy" whites indigenous to areas outside northern Europe. Deploring the influx of "Palatine Boors" into Pennsylvania, he found only "Saxons" to be acceptable as potential immigrants from Germany and favored England above all other sources of immigration.[302]

Thomas Paine, often cited as the most "leftist" of the American revolutionaries, called himself "a citizen of the world," and was not a racist. Even Paine, however, in his *Common Sense,* refers to America as the product of an ethnic core derived from the four closely related nations of England, Holland, Germany, and France.[303]

Thomas Jefferson, the outstanding liberal among the Founding Fathers, appreciated the value of ethnic homogeneity as the foundation of a politically stable nation and, therefore, advocated immigration restriction. The following excerpt from his *Notes on Virginia,* which he published in 1781, reveals that Jefferson sought to exclude immigrants from nations where serfdom and absolute monarchy were still entrenched:

> But are there no inconveniences to be thrown into the scale against any advantages expected from a multiplication of numbers by the importation of foreigners? It is for the happiness of those united in society to harmonize as much as possible in matters which of necessity they must transact together. Civil government being the sole object of forming societies, its administration must be conducted by common principles. Ours, perhaps, are more peculiar than those of any other. It is a composition of the freest principles of the English Constitution with others derived from natural right and natural reason. To these nothing can be more opposed than the maxims of absolute monarchies. Yet, from such we are to expect the greatest number of immigrants. They will bring with them the principles of the governments they leave, or if able to throw them off, it will be in exchange for an unbounded licentiousness, passing, as usual, from one extreme to the other. It would be a miracle were they to stop precisely at the point of temperate liberty. These principles, with their language, they will transmit to their children. In proportion to their number, they will infuse into it their spirit, warp or bias its direction, and render it a heterogeneous, incoherent, distracted mass.[304]

Among the conservative Founding Fathers, John Jay, writing in 1787 in the second paper of *The Federalist,* emphasizes ethnic unity as a source of the new nation's strength, giving thanks that "Providence has been pleased to give this one connected country to one united people, a people descended from the same ancestors, speaking the same language, professing the same religion, attached to the same principles of government, very similar in their manners and customs, and who, by their joint counsels, arms and efforts, fighting side by side throughout a long and bloody war, have nobly established general liberty and independence.'[305]

Writing eighty years after Jay, America's first political scientist, Francis Lieber, offered a definition of the nation which is similar in many particulars to that of Jay. Lieber also emphasized the nation's origin in an ethnic core. Lieber's definition of the nation was quoted, as follows, by Louis L. Snyder in 1990 in the latter's *Encyclopedia of Nationalism:*

> The word "nation," in the fullest adaptation of the term, means, in modern times, a numerous and homogeneous population (having long emerged from the hunters and nomadic' state), permanently inhabiting and cultivating a coherent territory, with a well-defined geographic outline, and a name of its own -- the inhabitants speaking their own language, having their own literature and common institutions, which distinguish them clearly from other and similar groups of people, being citizens or subjects of a unitary government, however subdivided it may be, and having an organic unity with one another as well as being conscious of a common destiny. Organic, intellectual and political internal unity with proportionate strength and a distinct and obvious demarcation from similar groups, are notable elements of the idea of a modern nation in its fullest sense.[306]

Not only is there considerable overlap between Jay's and Lieber's definitions, but they also parallel the definitions of ethnic groups which have been formulated by scholars more than a hundred years later. Anthony D. Smith, for example, writing in 1986 in his *The Ethnic Origins of Nations,* finds the core of a nation in what he calls "the ethnie." Ethnies are "human populations with shared ancestry myths, histories and cultures, having an association with a specific territory and a sense of solidarity." Uniting the ethnie is a "collective name," "imputed common ancestry and origins," and a shared culture which includes religion, language, customs, institutions, laws, folklore, architecture, dress, food, music, and arts. The sense of solidarity, "which in times of stress and danger can override class, factional or regional divisions within the community" partially explains why the "paradox of ethnicity is its mutability in persistence, and its persistence through change.'[307]

Gunnar P. Nillsson, writing in 1986 on "States and 'Nation-Groups': A Global Taxonomy," finds that "The characteristics connoted by *ethnic group* include such social category attributes as common racial identity, culture (including language and religion), kinship, social customs, history, and stable geographic contiguity . . . . A *nation-group* is an ethnic group that has become politically mobilized on the basis of ethnic group values . . . . *every ethnic group is a potential nation-group.*'[308] The "state-nation-group," called in German *das Staatsvolk,* exists "when one nation-group constitutes a majority of the population within a state.'[309]

Although written by various authors and over a period of two centuries, these definitions, when collated as follows, reveal a consensus regarding the attributes of a viable nation:

| | Jay | Lieber | Smith | Nillsson |
|---|---|---|---|---|
| 1. | common ancestry | homogeneous population | common ancestry | common racial identity |
| 2. | contiguous territory | coherent territory | specific territory | geographic contiguity |
| 3. | same language | own language | language | language |
| 4. | same religion | ———— | religion | religion |
| 5. | ———— | name of its own | collective name | ———— |
| 6. | manners & customs | literature & institutions | customs, etc. | social customs |
| 7. | same principles of government | unitary government | traditions of the community | *Staatsvolk* |
| 8. | joint triumph in war | conscious of common destiny | sense of solidarity | history |

Using this list, it is possible to assess the viability of the United States as a nation at different periods of its history. Arbitrarily taking the decades of the 1950s and the 1990s as two different reference points in time, and admitting that any such assessment must be impressionistic, the resulting inventory proceeds as follows:

1. The shift in the origins of the U.S. population is significant, from almost 90 percent of European descent in 1950 to only 75 percent so descended in 1990. After 1990, it is impossible to speak of "a typical American," much less to have in one's mind's eye an image of him (or her).

Writing in 1955, Will Herberg, a sociologist, defined the American self-image as follows:

The American's image of himself is still the Anglo-American ideal it was at the beginning of our independent existence. The "national type" as ideal has always been, and remains, pretty well fixed. It is the *Mayflower,* John Smith,

Davy Crockett, George Washington, and Abraham Lincoln that define the American's self-image, and this is true whether the American in question is a descendant of the Pilgrims or the grandson of an immigrant from southeastern Europe.[310]

Writing in 1984, one generation later, John Higham, the noted historian of immigration, described, as follows, the total fading out of the image described by Herberg:

> Cross-cut with memories of ancestral diversities, the host society becomes less and less capable of defining itself in an exclusive way. The Pilgrim and the Puritan have faded as American symbols. Craggy-featured Uncle Sam has gone too, and the Statue of Liberty has largely replaced Plymouth Rock. The newly minted term WASP became in the 1960's the only ethnic slur that could safely be used in polite company; for it was part of a largely successful assault on certain remaining bastions of ethnic exclusiveness.[311]

Neither Herberg nor Higham were writing as reactionary nativists. Herberg had made the difficult transition from Marxism to a neoconservatism based on traditional Judaism, while Higham was best-known for his unflattering portrayal of American nativists of all eras. More significant, of course, is the fact that the great deconstruction of American identity which is marked by the difference between these two accounts has not come to a halt in the 1990s, but has begun to accelerate.

2. The U.S. lost some contiguity of territory when it admitted Hawaii and Alaska to the Union as states. Having Hawaii and Alaska as defensive outposts should enhance the territorial integrity of the U.S. to whatever degree their distance from the mainland detracts from its contiguity. Complicating this assessment, however, was the independence movement which began to emerge in Hawaii in 1993, which had as one of its manifestations a refusal by the state's governor to fly the United States' flag over the Hawaiian capitol.[312] The Alaskan independence movement, which scored a symbolic victory with the election of the Alaskan Independence Party's gubernatorial candidate in 1992, represents a less serious unhappiness among Alaskans arising from the fact that most of the state's land is owned by the federal government.[313]

3. The difference between the decades is most striking in the area of language. In 1950, it was almost inconceivable that vast areas of the U.S. would ever again be functionally bilingual, as had been the case in some areas during the nineteenth century.

4. Significant differences are apparent between the two decades in the area of religion. All changes were in the direction of increased diversity, a weakened consensus, and a heightened potential for conflict.

Islam, almost unknown in the U.S. in 1950, after 1990 was becoming recognized in more areas as a community of faith no less significant than the Jewish, Protestant, and Catholic communities. Estimates of the number of Muslims in the U.S. varied, ranging from three million to six million, but everyone agreed that Islam was gaining in strength, having 250,000 adherents in just one state, Michigan. While popular journalism during the 1990s only tentatively began to enlarge "the Judaeo-Christian tradition" into a "Judaeo-Christian-Islamic tradition," references to "the three Abrahamic faiths" became more frequent.[314]

Islam has the potential to introduce a new factor into the political struggle over the separation of church and state. The imamate, unlike the Christian priesthood, has always been as much a secular as a sacred office. In fact, orthodox Islam recognizes no distinction between church and state, between the sacred and the secular. For this reason, the Muslims in what was once Yugoslavia, are recognized as a nationality group, and have suffered accordingly.[315]

Cults associated with the Third World, such as Santeria, flourish in the 1990s, but were almost unknown in 1950. Practitioners of Santeria, a variety of Afro-Cuban Voodoo which involves animal sacrifice, have come into conflict with local authorities in Florida and California. Some Santeria cultists, either motivated by criminal intent or under the influence of narcotic drugs, have committed murders and other heinous crimes.[316]

The heightened religious diversity of the 1990s made even more necessary than in the 1950s a thoroughgoing exclusion of religion from public life. Persons in public life knew that even the most innocuous references to the spiritual realm might promote inter-group conflict. Even an innocent reference to the fact that a majority of Americans still identified themselves as Christians could be seen as a demagogic appeal if uttered by an elected official. This heightened emphasis on the need for tolerance of all faiths had as its corollary an implication that no faith is to be taken seriously, an implied stance which promoted discontent among the devout of all faiths.

5. The U.S. has never had a true name of its own. There is a United Mexican States and a United States of Brazil, to be sure, but these are definite national names in a way that the United States of America is not. It was left to literary figures in the early republic to speculate about what the new nation should be called. Joel Barlow suggested Columbia, Edgar Allan Poe favored Appalachia. Others favored Alleghenia as a name. What is in a name? The citizens of the U.S. seem to have been successful in usurping for themselves the hemispheric label of American.

6. Manners and customs in the 1990s are retailed by way of the mass media and entertainment industries. Folk mores that were surviving feebly in 1950 were washed away by 1990. Among academicians, there was a struggle

during the 1990s to "define the canon of literary works." "Eurocentrism" in college reading lists seemed to be on the defensive. Western Civilization, as a course in the curriculum, seemed to be almost as endangered as Latin. Few people cared enough, however, to defend the traditional canon. One can only guess, but it seems unlikely that similar challenges to the common culture during the 1950s would have been met with the same acquiescence.

7. Principles of government seem to have been relatively unassailed, but a great shift is evident when one compares 1950 and 1990. States' rights continued to diminish. The executive arm of government continued to grow stronger. Ethnic representation began in the 1990s to challenge geographical representation in legislative bodies at all levels. The U.S. Constitution, however, seemed in the 1990s to be respected as little or as much as ever. It remained, of course, the document to which the U.S. Supreme Court invariably appealed whenever it wished to reverse some long-established contrary ruling. As the national political scripture, the Constitution still seemed capable of producing proof-texts for almost all arguments regarding public policy.

Nonetheless, behind the facade of law and order, there was evidence of the *de facto* reign of forces not acknowledged in the Constitution. The gap between the legal nation and the real nation had never been wider. Increasingly, the group, not the individual, was the fundamental unit of public policy. With the "War on Poverty," undertaken in response to widespread civil turmoil, the transition was completed which began with equal opportunity for individuals and ended with equal outcomes for groups. By the 1990s, the demand for equal outcomes had expanded beyond the economic realm to include the outcomes of elections for legislative and judicial offices and even the outcomes of jury trials. Silence about this great shift away from the constitutional philosophy of the Founding Fathers was, of course, but one more unspoken rule of daily life which was intended to keep consociational democracy functioning.

Smith and Nillsson, consciously defining nationhood from an ethnic perspective, present criteria in this category which slightly differ from those of Jay and Lieber, and by which the U.S. is found to be much more wanting in 1990 than in 1950. Community traditions are, after 1990, almost excluded from consideration in law. The American *Staatsvolk* in 1990, defined broadly to include all Americans having ancestors from northwestern and central Europe, still added up to a majority of the population, but it was banished from all mention in serious deliberations on public policy save as a party found to be collectively responsible for the most grievous of past wrongs.

The American *Staatsvolk* defined in narrower terms, as it was by the Founding Fathers, to include only Americans of British descent, was slightly less than twenty percent of the population in 1990. It may have been as much of a minority in 1950, but it is apparent that the "WASP" element had in that year a much greater impact on the nation's culture and, with it, its style of governance. By 1990, the ideals of the gentleman, of fair play, of sportsman-ship, ideals inherited from England, were practically extinct in the popular culture, recognized only to be derided as hypocrisy or weakness.

8. The final category seems to present four different values. These, how-ever, are linked as a common feeling among a nation's citizens that they live in "our country," not "this country" or "their country." It is that unconscious reaffirmation of unity, of consensus, of solidarity, of common destiny, of shared history -- John Stuart Mill's "fellow-feeling" -- manifested in count-less ways during every day of a nation's existence, which Ernest Renan, in the following words, defines as the very essence of nationhood:

> A nation is a grand solidarity constituted by the sentiment of sacrifices which one has made and those that one is disposed to make again. It supposes a past, it renews itself especially in the present by a tangible deed: the approval, the desire, clearly expressed, to continue the communal life. The existence of a nation is an everyday plebiscite.[317]

Again, comparisons must be conjectural, but it is likely that most serious observers of American life would agree that the affirmative vote in the daily plebiscite throughout the year 1950 was much higher than that during 1990. This is the decline of civic consensus to which Myrdal referred, midway between the two decades. It is likely, moreover, that the affirmative vote would continue to decline throughout the decades after 1990 even if the ethnic diversification of the U.S. were to be halted. The lack of an external enemy, the old Soviet Union, must lead to a decline in the fellow-feeling that was generated by a state of siege, the feeling of "us against them." In the 1990s and beyond, the feeling of "us against them" is more likely to be generated by confrontation with internal foes, not by one external enemy, a fellow-feeling which involves as much alienation from others as it involves identification with one's own kind.

The fragmenting or dissipation of American national unity, which is re-vealed in this survey of national characteristics, is traceable to a prior weaken-ing of the unity of the original ethnic core. This is the vital antecedent to nationhood and its abiding sustenance, in all of its cultural, legal, and histori-cal manifestations. As Emerich K. Francis defines it in his *Interethnic Rela-tions: An Essay in Sociological Theory*, "the nation is identified here not with the demotic unit of a given state population, but with an ethnic unit supposedly antedating any particular state."[318]

The ethnic core, although it seems to possess a life of its own apart from its manifestations, is not a mysterious thing-in-itself, like the folk-spirit of the Romanticists. It is definable as a kind of natural phenomenon. In the theory of the sociologist Frederik Barth,

> [E]thnic groups arise and persist by virtue of ''boundary creation and mainte-
> nance,'' . . . . Barth posits the concept of ethnicity to account for the presump-
> tive fact that groups persist through time in some integral, corporate fashion
> independently of, and in spite of, changes in the culture and institutions which
> the group circumscribes spatially and temporally . . . ethnicity is that dimen-
> sion of corporate identity that exists independently of any repertoire of cus-
> toms, beliefs, or institutions; because these are contingent and ever changing,
> they cannot account for group continuity and persistence. For a group to *have* a
> history and tradition, it must consist in some essential element *prior* to that
> history and tradition.[319]

To state that a nation and its ethnic core are natural phenomena is not to
equate either of them with a race. Reducing a nation to a race would be as
simplistic and flawed a procedure of definition as it would be to reduce a
nation to a state. The concepts race and nation exist in some relationship, but
are not identical. The relationship can be succinctly presented as follows: A
race precedes a nation and precedes even the formation of the ethnic core
which ''generates'' a nation. A race can appear in history in the guise of
numerous ethnic groups and nations. There is no one nation which in itself
constitutes a race.

The term race, imprecise and unscientific as commonly used, is derived
from the Italian *razza* and means simply, in the first definition given in the
*Oxford English Dictionary,* ''A group of persons, animals, or plants, connected by common descent or origin.'' The word may be used imprecisely and
poetically to refer to almost any line of descent; e.g., ''The race of Cain was
locked in a struggle for pre-eminence with the race of Seth.''

Taxonomists, those biologists who scientifically describe and classify living organisms, use other terms to describe the human taxa popularly known as
races. John R. Baker, reader in cytology at Oxford University, states that the
major divisions of humanity which have come to be known as races are, in
fact, subspecies. Humanity is but one species divided into subspecies as are
other species of mammals. Baker defines the taxa making up any one human
subspecies as races.[320] Nonetheless, the force of customary usage is such that
even Baker has entitled his definitive work on the topic simply *Race*.

A human subspecies is a natural phenomenon, unmodified in its genetic
nature by culture. While it may produce a culture, the reverse process cannot
occur. Even if, however, a subspecies were to be somehow modified by
culture, in the Lamarckian sense and against all hitherto observed evidence, it
would still be a natural phenomenon. Even if some future high culture
''creates'' a new human subspecies through eugenics or genetic engineering,

such a grand artifact will still be crafted in accord with natural laws. Culture itself is a product of natural laws. The fact that the complexity of culture exceeds the human capacity to describe it in quantitative terms as matter in motion, as scalars and vectors, does not mean that it is to be relegated to a domain exempt from natural laws. No matter how convoluted and massive a high culture may be, it is still subject to natural laws; it has not broken free from the chain of causality; not one of the concatenated links of cause and effect has been broken or ever will be.[321]

Although biologists have recognized that nations and ethnic groups represent complex phenomena which should be left to study by historians, sociologists, and cultural anthropologists, they have begun to study human behavior as a type of animal behavior. Ethology, the biological specialization which considers the innate behavioral tendencies or "biograms" of various species of animals, has provided a basis for a biological approach to the understanding of human behavior. Ethology won recognition as a science with the award, in 1973, of the Nobel Prize for Physiology and Medicine to ethologists Konrad Lorenz, Nikolaas Tinbergen, and Karl von Frisch. The works of several ethologists -- among them Jane Goodall, Konrad Lorenz, Desmond Morris, Lionel Tiger, and Robin Fox -- have become known to the general public outside the scientific community.[322]

Ethologists have centered their researches about three large areas of animal behavior: aggression, dominance, and territoriality. Simply stated, aggression is the mechanism which defines dominance, an individual's "rank" within the herd or group, as well as the limits of territory, the range upon which a band of animals feeds, either by predation or grazing.

Ethological data were gathered into a coherent body of knowledge by Edward O. Wilson, a professor of biology at Harvard University, and published in 1975 in his lengthy work, *Sociobiology; The New Synthesis. Sociobiology* became widely known as the name of a new field of scientific inquiry, an outgrowth of evolutionary biology and population biology, which Wilson has defined as "the systematic study of the biological basis of all social behavior."[323]

Territoriality is a biogram exhibited not simply by individual animals, mated pairs of animals, bands or herds or flocks of animals, but also by entire subspecies. Evolution itself largely proceeds by subspecific differentiation, a "successful" subspecies being one which "holds" the largest of territories. This is implicit in Wilson's definition of a subspecies, which he presents as follows in the opening pages of his work:

A population that differs greatly from other populations belonging to the same species is referred to as a *geographic race* or *subspecies*. Subspecies are separated from other subspecies by distance and geographic barriers that prevent the exchange of individuals, as opposed to the genetically basic "intrinsic isolating mechanisms" that hold species apart. Subspecies, insofar as they can be distinguished with any objectivity at all, show every conceivable degree of differentiation from other subspecies. At one extreme are the populations that fall along a cline -- a simple gradient in the geographic variation of a single character. In other words, a character that varies in a clinal pattern is one that changes gradually over a substantial portion of the entire range of the species. At the other extreme are subspecies consisting of easily distinguished populations that are differentiated from one another by numerous genetic traits and exchange genes across a narrow zone of intergradation.[324]

Human subspecies belong to the latter extreme, being both geographically distributed and differentiated by numerous genetic traits. The fact that a "zone of intergradation" exists between the populations of two subspecies does not mean that they are not "easily distinguished" as such. Desmond Morris defines these human subspecies and assesses their relative degrees of evolutionary "success" as follows:

The human species, as it began to spread out over the globe, started to form distinctive sub-species, just like any other animal. Three of these, the (white) Caucasoid group, the (black) Negroid group and the (yellow) Mongoloid group, have been highly successful. Two of them have not, and exist today as only remnant groups, shadows of their former selves. They are the Australoids -- the Australian Aborigines and their relatives -- and the Capoids -- the southern African bushmen. These two sub-species once covered a much wider range (the bushmen at one time owning most of Africa), but they have since been exterminated in all but limited areas.[325]

Morris describes and deplores the aggressive behavior which erupts when members of different human subspecies live within the same territory, particularly within the urbanized high cultures which he calls "the human zoo." He particularly emphasizes war, slavery, and rioting. Edward O. Wilson also deplores the fact that man's

. . . intergroup responses are still crude and primitive, and inadequate for the extended extraterritorial relationships that civilization has thrust upon him. The unhappy result is what Garrett Hardin has defined as tribalism in the modern sense . . . . Fearful of the hostile groups around them, the "tribe" refuses to concede to the common good. It is less likely to voluntarily curb its own population growth. Like the Sinhalese and Tamils of Ceylon, competitors may even race to outbreed each other. Resources are sequestered. Justice and liberty decline. Increases in real and imagined threats congeal the sense of group identity and mobilize the tribal members. Xenophobia becomes a political virtue.[326]

All of these responses, whether by conscious design or not, are directed to the ''success'' of one's group in an evolutionary sense; i.e., survival for one's group even if others must perish. This evolutionary-biological response may account for the fact that comparisons between groups are often considered more invidious than comparisons among individuals. This is noted by the sociologist Donald L. Horowitz, writing in his *Ethnic Groups in Conflict:* ''In interactions between groups, favoritism towards ingroups and discrimination against outgroups are demonstrated. What group members seem to desire is a positive evaluation of the group to which they belong. A favourable evaluation is attained by comparison to other groups in the environment.''[327]

Though deploring ethnocentrism, many sociobiologists agree that it may be best understood in terms of the phenomenon in evolutionary biology which W.D. Hamilton has called ''inclusive fitness.'' This concept is defined by the editors of *The Sociobiology of Ethnocentrism,* a collection of papers delivered in 1985 at a conference of the European Sociobiological Society, as follows:

> . . . . Inclusive fitness theory, . . . shows that genes will spread if their carriers act to increase not only their own fitness or reproductive success but also that of other individuals carrying the same genes . . . . We can assume that for most of human evolution those genes survived whose bearers achieved the greatest inclusive fitness, i.e. whose behaviour was not just selfishly reproductive and promoted the survival of their own children, but was also socially helpful to the reproductive success of relatives such as brothers, sisters, cousins, nephews and nieces, all of whom carried proportions of their own genes . . . . Ethnocentrism could thus be the extension in humans of the distinctive psychobiology of those species in which there is an active social family life.[328]

Ethnocentric individuals, by contributing to the survival of even distantly related individuals, which members of the same subspecies are, promote the survival of their own genes. This, of course, is a matter of natural selection, neither a conscious process nor the emergence of some teleological design within nature. Ira Silverman, writing in the same work on ''Inclusive Fitness and Ethnocentrism,'' explains, as follows, how inclusive fitness is applicable to a large group beyond the extended family:

> The arithmetical framework of kin selection and inclusive fitness renders these concepts, in fact, readily extrapolable to ethnocentrism, in that ethnic attitudes and behaviours seem to be most salient when large groups are involved. A seemingly ''negligibly small'' coefficient of relationship between two individuals will sum to a significant level across several hundreds or thousands. Thus, though it may not sufficiently serve one's fitness to sacrifice for another who is perceived as sharing a coefficient of relationship of 1/1000, the gains from helping 500 such individuals may begin to approximate those

achieved by nepotism. Similarly, twice the gain in fitness is realised by favouring a group whose members are perceived to bear coefficients of relationship of 1/1000, over a group whose members bear perceived coefficients of 1/2000.[329]

Robin J.H. Russell, writing on ''Genetic Similarity as a Mediator of Interpersonal Relationships,'' reports that ''a number of animal species have been shown to be able to detect degree of genetic similarity to others and to adjust their behavior appropriately.'' He concludes regarding inclusive fitness that ''the theory suggests that members of different groups are more likely to have aggressive encounters and less likely to be kind to each other than members of the same group.''[330]

Colin J. Irwin, reporting on ''A Study in the Evolution of Ethnocentrism'' among Eskimo tribes, applies quantitative methods to his data to test the inclusive fitness theory and concludes that ''Humans are genetically predisposed to ethnocentrism.'' He qualifies this statement, however, by adding that ''The corollary of ethnocentrism, xenophobia, a fear of strangers, is likewise provided with an evolutionary explanation. Predisposed has a similar meaning to innate and needs to be qualified, as the development of ethnocentric behaviours will be greatly affected by the developmental environment of individuals.''[331]

Heiner Flohr's ''Biological Bases of Social Prejudices'' examines the origin of prejudiced and stereotypical thinking as evolutionary mechanisms, not simply the belated products of culture. Flohr cites Rupert Riedl who ''has pointed to the enormous role that pre-judgments play in the behaviour of all living systems . . . . Pre-judgments are, according to Riedl, a precondition for our existence. As long as they are more likely than a random search to lead to correct judgments, thereby protecting the conditions of survival, they are functional.''[332] Stereotypical thinking, in particular the tendency to dichotomize, arises because ''Our way of thinking has developed as a response to practical problems of living and not as an optimal solution to finding the truth. Therefore we tend to think more in terms of categories or classes than in terms of individuals . . . . Using these generalizations we form schemata.'' Though ''extremely useful,'' ''they enable us to form stereotypes . . . . In politics this tendency leads to a radical thinking in opposite terms, like friend versus foe.''[333]

Flohr argues that there is a biological basis for xenophobia and considers, as follows, the common objections to that theory:

. . . . Xenophobia seems to be universal, i.e. it seems to occur in all cultures. This is no proof but strong evidence in favour of a biological basis of xenophobia.

Another argument in favour of a biological basis of xenophobia is the apparently innate fear of strangers that can be observed in little children . . . . Infants turn away from strangers, avoid eye contacts with them and start to cry when they are touched by strange persons . . . .

There are a number of objections against the assumption that the rejection of strangers is innate . . . . However, neither the fact that the timing of this behaviour differs between individuals, nor individual differences in the strength of this behaviour, nor the mixture of rejection with signs of cautious interest can cast serious doubt on the core of the argument that the rejection of strangers is innate. Besides, such individual differences and the mixture of fear and curiousness can also be observed in animals. Aggression against strangers in animals could correlate negatively with the degree of genetic relationship, and this would of course fit into the theoretical framework presented by sociobiology (cf. Hamilton 1975). However that may be, it seems warranted to assume that xenophobia is innate in all animal species characterized by complex social organization (E.O. Wilson 1975) and thus also in man.[334]

Wolfgang Toennesmann considers nations in the light of inclusive fitness theory in his "Group Identification and Political Socialisation" and asserts that "both selfishness and altruism are part of human nature," despite the reluctance of social scientists to accept the concept of human nature. In the following concluding remarks, he addresses social scientists in particular, but his observations are salient for all who are concerned with public policy:

. . . . the propensity of people in the modern world to identify with groups, and in particular with their own nation or ethnic group, may be understood in evolutionary terms as an element in the set of evolutionary selected propensities called human nature. There are good reasons to assume not only that the human capacity for culture has evolved biologically . . . , but that this evolution occurred together with the evolution of particular traits of human social behaviour, such as the propensity to become attached to groups and to draw a sharp line between in-groups and out-groups. Such a human-nature argument may be regarded as irrelevant by those whose interest it is to find out *when* something will occur and *how* this occurrence can be modified rather than being told that something *can* occur because it is part of the evolutionary selected behavioural repertoire . . . . In view of the fact, however, that social scientists have often failed with regard to these seemingly simpler tasks of predicting when and how something will occur, it may not be a bad idea to consult other fields in a search for information on what can be expected of human behaviour in the long run . . . .[335]

The division between in-group and out-group, the ubiquity of dual systems of ethics, xenophobia and violence in the partitioning of territory are all phenomena that are, of course, well-known to historians. Even the best-known work of history, the Mosaic books of the Old Testament, is little more than an account of such phenomena, which are there represented as ordained by a supreme being. Wilson has noted that Moses, when his people conquered the Midianites, gave them "instructions identical in result to the aggression and genetic usurpation by male langur monkeys."[336] Moses' commands to the conquering Israelites were: "Now therefore kill every male among the little ones, and kill every woman that hath known a man by lying with him. But all the women children, that have not known a man by lying with him, keep alive for yourselves." (See Numbers 31:17-18; King James Version.)

Territoriality among human subspecies has been given an unflinching examination by E. Raymond Hall, professor of biology at the University of Kansas, whose *The Mammals of North America,* published in its second edition in 1981, remains the definitive reference work in its field.[337] Hall's article, "Zoological Subspecies of Man," presents candidly in the following paragraph the unembellished facts regarding territoriality among subspecies:

> . . . . Consider, if you will, the results of competition between closely allied subspecies of wild mammals when one penetrates into or is introduced into the range of another. Whether they be mice, moles, or monkeys, one and only one subspecies survives in a given area, because after a few thousand years, ordinarily in a much shorter time, crossbreeding may result in amalgamation, a sort of extinction by dilution. But the more common results are either that they fight and one kills the other, or that as a result of less direct combat, the individuals of one subspecies more often usurp the best food, places best suited for rearing young, and shelters affording maximum protection from enemies. Therefore the one subspecies thrives, whereas the other subspecies because of lower birth rate and decreased longevity that result from inferior food, inferior nurseries and insufficient shelter, decreases and disappears. The introduced black rat *(Rattus rattus rattus)* has disappeared from some large areas in North America where competition was furnished by another subspecies, *Rattus rattus alexandrinus.* So it goes in almost every instance where kinds of mammals so closely related as subspecies of the same species are suddenly thrown into competition over a large area. Indeed, study of the thousands of subspecies of native wild mammals has led to the formulation of the biological law concerning them that: *Two subspecies of the same species do not occur in the same geographic area.* Of the half dozen or fewer exceptions reported to date, reinvestigation has shown that the two kinds instead were in every instance full species, or two subspecies that lived each in a habitat apart from the other. Thus the rule remains almost or quite without exception and it should give pause to anyone about to advocate the long continued residence together of subspecies of man.[338]

Territoriality among human subspecies is continental in its scope. The implications, which Hall presents as follows, are thought-provoking:

Another zoological generalization that man ought to take into account is that when two kinds of closely related animals are thrown into competition, the one native to the larger land mass ordinarily prevails. The reported increase of the introduced Old World reindeer *(Rangifer tarandus tarandus)* in Alaska at the expense of the native caribou *(Rangifer tarandus arcticus)* is a case in point. The red-backed mouse *(Clethrionomys dawsoni),* which seems to be relatively a newcomer to the Alaskan area of North America from Asia, appears to be succeeding at the expense of the native American red-backed mouse *(Clethrionomys gapperi).* In past geological ages there have been several interchanges of fauna between North America and Asia. These were at times when a higher land level, or a lower sea level, between Asia and North America provided a land bridge between those two continents. Our increasingly complete record of fossil mammals shows that the balance in those past ages, as well as in the present, definitely favored the large land mass, Asia . . . . That is to say, of the mammals that North America gave to Asia in later geologic time only the camels and horses survived there; but of the mammals that Asia gave to North America, elk, moose, reindeer, bison, and other species prevailed and remain in North America today.

What, then, are the chances of survival of the Caucasians in North America if they permit the infiltration of the Oriental subspecies of man from the larger land mass of Asia? The Caucasians' chances would appear poor indeed. But the Caucasians are not Americans -- there isn't a family among them that can claim residence of more than 400 years on this continent; the Caucasians, too, are from the larger land mass, the Asiatic land mass, albeit from its western edge whereas the Orientals are from its eastern edge. What the Caucasian subspecies did to the subspecies native here, the American Indian, whose ancestors at a much earlier time came from Asia, the Caucasians may after all avoid for themselves because their recent Asiatic origin gives them in North America almost a 50-50 chance with the Orientals.

But, is this competition necessary? To invite it by permitting the immigration of Orientals, and to foster it by granting citizenship on the North American mainland to Orientals seems foolish and violates every biological law, of recent and past geological ages, that relates to the harmonious existence of two or more subspecies of the same species. To imagine one subspecies of man living together on equal terms for long with another subspecies is but wishful thinking and leads only to disaster and oblivion for one or the other. More to the point at the moment, such a course and its inescapable consequence insure in the process of solution either bloodshed and violence or a more insidious competition in which racial prejudice, and fancied superiority, set over against alleged inferiority, come to the surface with all of the associated evils that poison men's minds, sicken their bodies and torture their souls.[339]

An escape from the grim vision which Hall presents might seem to be offered by the alternative in which different subspecies blend into a dilution of their characteristics so that individuals cannot be assigned to any one subspecies. This is, in Edward O. Wilson's terms, the "narrow zone of intergradation" which arises between subspecies having territories which overlap to a limited extent. Hall also refers to "intergradation," citing as an example "a belt of transition" in Asia where most of the inhabitants are "intergrades" between Caucasians and "Orientals (subspecies *asiaticus)."*[340] The probability that this alternative can offer an escape from America's dilemma seems, however, to be lessened because intergradation is, according to Hall, the less common outcome of a meeting of subspecies, while Wilson describes the zone of intergradation as being "narrow."

The devolution of the USSR into, among other newly organized states, Russia and Kazakhstan, is but more evidence of the principle that the masses of two neighboring subspecies will seek to follow separate paths which lead them into separate territories. Russia, of course, is overwhelmingly Caucasian, while Kazakhstan is best described as the state of "intergrades," the zone of intergradation to which Hall refers. Thus, it may not be unjustified to argue that racism was one important factor among the many which doomed the old Soviet Union. (This interpretation assumes, of course, that the inexorable tendency of two distinct subspecies to seek two distinct territorial ranges is a manifestation of racism, albeit separatist rather than supremacist.)[341]

It can be argued that the Soviet Union acted as an heir to the old racist-colonialist ideology of "the white man's burden." Samuel P. Oliner, professor of sociology at Humboldt State University, writing in 1987, prior to the dissolution of the USSR, observed that "Western scholars are skeptical of . . . optimistic claims of assimilation and racial and ethnic amalgamation, known respectively as *sblizhenie* and *slivanie,* or the drawing and merging together of ethnic groups under the Russian banner.''[342] Oliner calls the Central Asian republics "internal colonies," and quotes Rocky L. Rockett's *Ethnic Nationalities in the Soviet Union,* as follows: "Both the internal colonial and the classical colonial approaches are most applicable in cases where racial and cultural differences are extreme. In the case of the Soviet Union, the Slavic/Muslim cultural contrast is sufficient to warrant an analysis of the relationship between these two groups of people from a colonial perspective.''[343]

It can also be argued that Russia and the other Slavic republics elected the separatist-racist option by rejecting a future of intergradation and founding new states largely limited to the subspecies *Homo sapiens europaeus* (i.e., Caucasians in the Linnaean nomenclature). Although this is not the thesis of Teresa Rakowska-Harmstone, a professor of political science at Canada's Carleton University, she suggests, writing in 1992 in the *Journal of International Affairs,* a similar motivation in stating that Yeltsin's formation of the Commonwealth of Independent States "was undoubtedly prompted by Russia's desire to safeguard its interests and influence throughout the key parts of the old union. One also suspects that the prospect of supporting the economically bankrupt Muslim republics as Russia's sole remaining partners of the old union was behind Yeltsin's effort to rebuild ties with the other Slavs."[344]

Russia's decision to shed its colonies, to drop the "white man's burden," was hastened when even the affirmative action program initiated in 1983 by Yuri Andropov failed to appease the restive Asian republics. Rakowska-Harmstone analyzes the shift in Russian thinking as follows:

> Troublesome as the emergence of nationalism among the non-Russians proved to be in the late 1970s and the early 1980s, it was not in itself a threat to the stability of the Soviet state. The decisive variable was the growth of Russian nationalism, which was revived partly in response to the demands of the minorities, but largely because of a dawning perception that the Russians had been ill-used by the system. A watershed came sometime in the 1970s, when more and more Russians began to feel that the interests of the Soviet state and the interests of the Russian nation no longer coincided and began to question the assumption that they ever had. The new perception of a threat to their political status in the non-Russian republics was joined by a perception of a threat to their biological survival, in view of demographic trends and indicators of environmental destruction. The Russians developed a resentment of the sacrifices they felt they had made in fulfilling their role as an elder brother for which they were repaid with ingratitude. They felt that they had been exploited by a system based on an alien ideology, which had attempted to destroy the very essence of Russian culture and spiritual values.[345]

Viewed from this perspective, Boris Yeltsin is the most benign as well as the easternmost of the "nationalist demagogues" against whom Erazim Kohak has warned. He was most benign because all that was needed to produce a new republic largely limited to *europaeus* was a simple separation, a relatively bloodless operation compared to the violence, often lethal, which was being employed in the newly reunited Germany at the same time in order to preserve it, too, as the territory of but one subspecies. Admittedly simplistic, this interpretation nonetheless accords with Hall's two major observations that (1) two mammalian subspecies do not coexist in the same territory for long, and (2) intergradation is the least often elected resolution of the conflict arising from the coexistence of two mammalian subspecies within the same territory.

Hall notes (on p. 7) that intergradation has been most successful in the United States between *Homo sapiens americanus* and *Homo sapiens europaeus*. He maintains that only the system of reservations gave the former subspecies the territory it needed to save itself from utter extermination. The outcome was, however, a happy one. Descendants of Caucasians who sought to kill all Indians were themselves eager to claim Indian ancestry, as is revealed by the quantum leap of Americans reporting Indian ancestry in the decennial census. According to the latter, Americans of Indian ancestry increased in number from a mere one-half of a million in 1960 to almost two million in 1990.

At first glance it would seem that such an intergradation offers the best hope for peace among the various human subspecies in the United States. It would mean that the U.S., or a portion of its territory, a kind of MexAmerican Kazakhstan, would be added to the vast zone of intergrades *(mestizos)* which have long inhabited America south of the Rio Grande. The Mexican philosopher Jose Vasconcelos saw in this developing zone of intergradation the wave of the future, a future humanity whose advent he heralded in 1925 in his essay, *La Raza Cosmica*.

Even Mexico, however, was by the end of the twentieth century far from being the homeland of a new cosmic race. As Lester Langley notes in his *MexAmerica*, northern Mexico is Caucasian Mexico while southernmost Mexico is Indian Mexico. Intergrades, the *Mestizos*, may be found everywhere, but the strongholds of the distinct subspecies remain, albeit tenuously. Alan Riding, in his *Distant Neighbors*, notes a fundamental ambivalence among European Mexicans regarding the nation's Indian past. In Guadalajara, Mexico's second largest city, "Outsiders -- *mestizos*, Jews and Arabs -- are generally unwelcome in aristocratic circles, but French and Spanish migrants are accepted as contributing to the 'whiteness' of the city."[346] Riding sums up Mexican ambivalence thusly: "Proud of its Indian past, Mexico seems ashamed of its Indian present."[347] He notes that Benito Juarez remains the nation's "only pure-blooded Indian president."[348]

Brazil, in the popular mind, is the true homeland of the cosmic race, a paragon of inter-group relations where three different human subspecies are soon to melt away into intergradation. Something approaching this vision was carried in the minds of the UNESCO investigators who visited Brazil early in the 1950s, hoping to learn the secret of inter-group amity. Their report reflected their confrontation with a reality quite contrary to all anticipations. It had been long known that Brazil's ruling elite had been influenced by racist ideology, but it still came as a great disillusionment to discover that racism permeated the thinking of the masses of the Brazilian people.[349]

It has been theorized that what appears to be racism in Brazil is really a form of class prejudice descending from the days of slavery in that country. This notion has been challenged, however, by several carefully researched studies reported in *Race, Class and Power in Brazil*, a symposium published in 1985 by the Center for Afro-American Studies at the University of California-Los Angeles. Carlos A. Halsenbalg, writing on "Race and Socioeconomic Inequalities in Brazil," concludes that "Almost nine decades after the abolition of slavery, Brazilian blacks and mulattos are still concentrated at the bottom of the social hierarchy. Compared to whites, the greater part of the nonwhite population lives in the least developed regions of the country."[350] Nelson do Valle Silva, writing on "Updating the Cost of Not Being White in Brazil," presents data which explode the favored theory of a "mulatto escape-hatch," the notions that "mulattos are expected to attain higher educational, occupational, and economic levels" and that "race plays no significant role in the process of mobility."[351] Do Valle Silva's studies, based on the 1960 and 1976 census data, "found that Blacks and mulattos seem to display unexpectedly similar profiles. In this respect nonwhites clearly contrast with whites, and thus to speak of a 'nonwhite' racial group does no violence to reality."[352]

Pierre-Michel Fontaine, the editor, notes in his "Introduction" that "The vote for Black candidates, if not the Black vote, appears to be small."[353] To overcome their political weakness, black Brazilians have launched their own Black Power movement. According to Anani Dzidzienyo, professor of Afro-American Studies at Brown University, the Indians in Brazil have failed to unite politically. The government's professed aim of "integration" of the Indians is a strategy by which "the Indian can be virtually defined out of existence rather than being exterminated."[354] The fact that Europeans such as Juscelino Kubitschek and Ernesto Geisel have risen to the presidency of Brazil, but never a black or an Indian, is indicative. Further complicating Brazil's ethnic situation were one million Asian Brazilians, who in 1990 were reported as having the highest incomes of all ethnic groupings in the country.[355]

Brazil's most popular celebrity in the early 1990s was "Xuxa," the stage name of a blond-haired, blue-eyed daughter of Italian, Polish, and German immigrants. "You have a nation that is half brown or black, and the national symbol is blond. Our culture is profoundly racist," said Herbert de Souza, a Brazilian sociologist. Abdias do Nascimento, a leader in Brazil's United Black Movement, said of the Xuxa phenomenon that "It's very negative for children. It makes people despise themselves . . . . You have little black girls who only want blond dolls."[356]

Brazil's industrially and politically powerful south is the home of its unmixed European population, which includes two million unassimilated Germans. A poll taken in 1993 revealed that a third of the 22 million people living in the southernmost three provinces would favor secession from Brazil to form a new Republic of the Pampas. *The New York Times,* in a story headlined "White Flight in Brazil? Secession Caldron Boils," reported that several secession groups were active and focused on the Farroupilha Republic Party and one of its spokesmen, Irton Marx. Although some Brazilians have accused the secessionists of being "racist," they have claimed a purely economic motivation for their movement, stressing that they have been funneling trillions of cruzeiros into the Amazon and the northeast. According to a secessionist pamphlet, which presents an argument similar to that of the advocates of a Northern California, the Brazilian government returns to the south only 63 percent of the federal revenues which it collects from the south.[357] Despite its denial of racism, the secessionist movement would sever an area which is 85 percent European from the overwhelmingly black northeast and the overwhelmingly Indian Amazon region.

Brazil, like other multi-ethnic states, is far from being a "universal nation." It is, in fact, but one more area of the earth's surface where contention among different human subspecies is at least as significant as intergradation. There is much intergradation in Brazil's population, but it is also evident that the country has great numbers of three different human subspecies which are entrenched in three different territorial strongholds. Even if the movement to establish a separate Republic of the Pampas fails, the fact that such a movement can even arise provides yet more evidence that a "universal nation" is a contradiction in terms, almost as impossible as a conical sphere. If ethnicity, ethnocentrism, and racism have not begun to subside in Brazil, then where in the world will they subside?

Uruguay, immediately south of Brazil, has been called the Switzerland of South America and prides itself on its tradition of being a haven for political refugees. Nonetheless, this tolerance does not extend to the 180,000 blacks among the country's three million people, according to a report appearing in 1993 in *The New York Times*. Several organizations have appeared in recent years attempting to combat "an unspoken discrimination" against blacks and to improve their socio-economic status. Uruguay has no black members of Congress, no black labor leaders, and only fifty black professionals. "Seventy-five percent of our women are maids," said Romero Rodriguez, head of Afro Mundo, the most radical among the black groups. "We get the worst jobs. We live in the most marginal areas. The only reference in textbooks is that blacks came here as slaves."[358]

Latin America, defined as the whole expanse from the Rio Grande to Tierra del Fuego, is far from being one great zone of intergradation and farther still from being the homeland of the cosmic race. Carlton Beals, writing in 1938 in his *America South*, described the basic racial-geographic contours of this vast land in terms of three large population areas, as follows:

(1) a vast highland-tropic Indian-mestizo empire, from Arizona, New Mexico, part of Texas, through Mexico and Central America, with a white Danzig corridor of Costa Rica, through the Andean region on down to Paraguay; (2) the present European Latin states of Argentina and Chile; (3) a vast mulatto element stretching from Brazil north through all the Caribbean, trying to drive a wedge into Panama, and Honduras, and fringing all the coasts, except that of Mexico, taking in the islands (a minority in the Dominican Republic), and absorbing the lower tier of the American states.[359]

"Regrouped," Beals describes Argentina, Uruguay, Chile, southern Brazil, and Costa Rica as "White"; "all tropic-highland regions, including Panama, excluding Costa Rica," as "Mestizo-Indian"; and "northern Brazil, Caribbean islands and coasts of Central America, Colombia, Venezuela" as "Mulatto-zambo-Negro."[360] A 1974 survey of Latin America, published by the British Broadcasting Corporation, includes a map of "racial distribution," which confirms Beals' description. The map reveals strongholds where one subspecies *(Homo sapiens afer)* predominates in northeast Brazil, another *(Homo sapiens europaeus)* in the whole area from southern Brazil to Tierra del Fuego, and yet a third *(Homo sapiens americanus* in the interiors of South America and of Mexico. Zones of intergradation, not shown on the map, but accounted for in Beals' description, surround the stronghold areas.[361]

One factor which strongly militates against intergradation as a solution to inter-group conflict in the United States is the emphasis which is given to group identity in almost all aspects of governmental policy. "Statistical Policy Directive No. 15: Race and Ethnic Standards for Federal Statistics and Administrative Reporting," published by the President's Office of Management and Budget, describes groupings which, in four out of five instances, parallel in all but name the human subspecies recognized by taxonomy. The federal categories and the corresponding human subspecies, using the Linnaean terms, are as follows:

| **Directive 15** | **Human Subspecies** |
| --- | --- |
| American Indian or Alaskan Native | *Homo sapiens americanus* |
| Asian or Pacific Islander | *Homo sapiens asiaticus* |
| Black, not of Hispanic origin | *Homo sapiens afer* |
| Hispanic | ———————— |
| White, not of Hispanic origin | *Homo sapiens europaeus* |

Hispanics, of course, include members of the human subspecies *americanus, afer,* and *europaeus,* as well as various intergrades.

Intergradation as the prevailing option for America's future appears to be unlikely not only because it is less often chosen by individuals of separate subspecies when they come into confrontation, but also because the federal government is actually campaigning against it. Instances of an individual's falsely claiming some fraction of non-European descent in order to win promotion in the civil service or the award of a federal contract are becoming increasingly common. Although it must be admitted that such an assessment cannot be quantitatively demonstrated, it is likely that in a single day of the operation of its program of affirmative action and minority-owned business "set-asides," the federal government does more to promote race-consciousness among European Americans than the combined efforts throughout the years of all of the so-called "hate groups."

Each individual's identification with a particular subspecies is being reinforced in every case save that of the Hispanics, who are a cultural grouping lumped into one body by the federal government for the sake of administrative convenience. Even the Hispanic identity, manifold as it is, but mostly an identity of intergrades, has political reinforcement. Individuals in the Hispanic group are unlikely to seek a "transfer," even if it were possible, to another group. Hence, Hispanics lose the preeminent role which they otherwise might play of being the vanguard population leading a general drift towards intergradation.

Human subspecies are, of course, the groupings which Gordon Allport identifies as macrodiacritic and pandiacritic. Their mobilization into political conflict groups is readily effected. Indeed, that very possibility seems to be the one great fear among American governing circles. However, their demobilization so that they might become the rational, individual citizens of a constitutional republic may not be so easily effected, particularly in a society where there is a limited supply of the most desired and necessary goods and resources. Those who give heed to the findings of ethology and sociobiology should also give a second thought to any aspect of governmental policy which, intentionally or otherwise, politically mobilizes groupings of humanity which are predisposed to seek separate territorial ranges.

Ethologists and sociobiologists have delivered the unwelcome message that ethnocentrism and racism are not simply social problems, but also natural phenomena. Unhappiness over what they have reported has been so intense that many people have displaced their reactions into anger at the messengers who brought the unpleasing news or else have retreated from any confrontation with the facts into the time-honored denial which asserts that humanity is not part of nature, but is somehow above nature and beyond its laws. This insistence on regarding humans as some species of supranatural beings is found among both the devout and the secular, among both the idealistic few and the practical many who cannot be bothered with theory, and among adherents at both ends of the traditional left-right political spectrum.

Heiner Flohr cites this false dichotomy between nature and culture as an example of humanity's innate tendency to think in stereotypes. It is certainly the favored stereotype among those who evince an almost panicky hatred of even the concept that there can be a human nature anterior to culture. All of the angry denial probably arises from an awareness that the very notion of a human nature understandable in terms of evolutionary biology deals the blow of mercy to the dying system of Marxism, including its Freudianized variants,

which, in any case, has proven powerless to explain the eruption of ethnocentrism in the very heartland of Marxism.

Despite the outrage it provokes, sociobiology makes clearer the meaning of
what John Stuart Mill vaguely described as the "fellow-feeling" which must
exist for a nation to be viable. Ernest Renan's definition of nationhood is even
more meaningful when considered in the light of sociobiology. Renan's
central concepts of a "grand solidarity," "an everyday plebiscite," "the
desire to continue the communal life" are revealed to be humanistic synonyms
for the sociobiological concept of inclusive fitness. Sociobiology has pointed
to the very life's well of the nation's being, its basic sustenance in evolving
life, anterior to but not apart from culture. Although the state may be the
highest artifact of human culture, it will be most readily sustained, nurtured,
promoted, and defended when it is rooted in and the expression of an ethnically whole nation.

# VIII

## The Outlook for America

I t is often argued that Americans, as a matter of principle, may not restrict immigration because America is a nation of immigrants. That, however, is true of any nation. The inhabitants of all areas of the earth's surface have at least some antecedents who migrated there at some time in past ages. The whole Western Hemisphere was first populated at a comparatively recent time when people from Asia migrated across an isthmus that later became the Bering Straits. In the Western Hemisphere, Canada and Argentina are also nations of immigrants.

Simply because the United States or some other nation has had a massive influx of immigrants in the past is no reason for that policy to be continued in the future. The suggestion that because something once was, it must always be is an example of a flaw in logic, the *non sequitur,* which particularly plagues discussions of the immigration question. The argument that American citizens who favor the exclusion of aliens must also hate them is another example of the same flawed logic. The one assertion does not necessarily follow from the other. Most of the other objections to immigration restriction are based on this fallacy.

America's history as a nation of immigrants is not unique. What is unique is the extent to which America has opened itself to immigration. In the 1990s, the United States admits as many immigrants each year as do all other countries in the world combined. This remarkable disproportion had its origins in the era when the United States was as yet thinly populated, in comparison with the European nations, and when the U.S. had rapidly growing industries which readily employed the newcomers. Such conditions simply do not exist in the 1990s.

As early as the last decade of the nineteenth century, the U.S. had begun to suffer from overcrowding in the cities of its Northeast, an overcrowding which produced slums as squalid as any in Europe. Jacob Riis's pioneering work in photojournalism, *How the Other Half Lives,* published in 1890, is the classic examination of the problem. A flood of immigrants, sometimes exceeding a million per year, literally swamped available housing. Despite the publicity given to the ugly new phenomenon of the American slum tenement, massive immigration was allowed to continue until it was largely interrupted by World War I. Supposedly, immigrants were needed to work in growing industries.

Legislation restricting immigration was slow in being enacted although millions of Americans as early as the 1850s favored such restriction. Nativist organizations enrolled millions of members dedicated to the cause of immigration restriction, but legislation which significantly limited the numbers of immigrants did not become a reality until the 1920s. The cause of this lag is not at all mysterious. It inhered in the simple fact that legislators put foremost the interests of employers who sought an abundant supply of labor. A copious supply of any commodity, which labor is when considered from the employers' standpoint, can always be purchased cheaply.

At the end of the twentieth century, the overwhelming majority of legislators still do not emerge from the class of employees. Although nine-tenths of the households represented by elected officials are dependent on salaries and wages, the overwhelming majority of elected officials are self-employed when they are elected to office, belonging to a class representing less than a tenth of the population. Most of them, moreover, are lawyers or businessmen active in commerce or finance. People in the latter fields have perennially welcomed almost any factor increasing the population of the U.S. More people, in their eyes, represent more clients, customers, and borrowers. For most legislators, immigrants do not represent fellow slum-dwellers, fellow-homeless, or even competitors for employment.

Even the most liberal of public officials, those who are ready to express concern for the plights of slum-dwellers, the homeless, and the unemployed, have themselves not been above employing undocumented, illegal aliens because they have been able to avoid paying them the higher wages and fringe benefits which a citizen might earn. Early in 1993, public outrage erupted upon the discovery of one such instance involving a nominee for appointment as the Attorney General of the U.S.

Given the perennial shortsightedness among the American elite regarding the effects of massive immigration, the period of limited immigration, barely more than four decades from 1924 to 1965, was an exceptional period, one time when the elite finally responded to the nativist sentiments of the American majority. Previous laws limiting immigration had been directed only at certain populations, such as Asian contract laborers, paupers, criminals, the illiterate or insane, but the act of 1924 established a comprehensive system of quotas based on the national origins of the U.S. population. Only a few years after its enactment, the U.S. plunged into the Great Depression, followed by World War II, two prolonged crises which alone would have acted to curtail immigration.

This fortuitous period afforded an all-important interlude when the assimilative powers of the nation were able to effect some acculturation of the masses of immigrants who had arrived during the previous century. The assimilation that was accomplished, however, as has been noted previously, was facilitated by the fact that almost all of the immigrants were microdiacritic Europeans. Generally, the disappearance of separate foreign-language institutions was followed, within another generation, by the disappearance of most other separatist ethnic institutions.

The factors which produced this great interruption in the immigrant influx -- a nativist upsurge, depression, and two world wars -- may or may not recur in the twenty-first century to produce another long period of restricted immigration. Assuming such events do not occur, however, the likelihood that legislators will move to curtail immigration and effectively patrol America's borders depends on convincing them that it is necessary for the good of the country in both the near and the distant future. The good of the country includes, of course, but is not limited to, a continuance of its tradition of constitutional governance.

If the immigrant influx into the U.S. is not curtailed, then not only will assimilation continue to fail and go into retrograde motion, becoming affirmative ethnicity and separatism, but the country will suffer from political conflict and civil strife to an unprecedented degree. The U.S. is becoming far too crowded with people, as is evidenced by urban problems in general and the problem of the homeless in particular. Moreover, American industries in the 1990s are no longer growing at a rapid rate. Growth is negligible at best. More and more capital is being exported across the southern border into Mexico or into other Third World nations. Decades of rising expectations have given way to a decade of "plateaued" expectations, and will be succeeded by decades of declining expectations in reaction to a lowering of the average person's standard of living. Given continued immigration, there will soon be too many people demanding too few goods and natural resources. Conflict everywhere will be the result.

This is the unwelcome reality which lurks behind the report of the U.S. Census Bureau that, given a continuation of the levels of immigration reached during the 1990s, there will be almost 400 million people in the U.S. by 2050. Massive immigration, if continued, will bring about a rapid growth of population in the U.S. at a time when the European nations and Japan have long ago controlled their numbers. Japan, in particular, is an example of a nation which has prospered by limiting its population, excluding almost all immigrants, and employing robotics in lieu of importing cheap labor. Burgeoning populations anywhere in the contemporary world, including the U.S., mean a growth in social problems at the very time when resources for their solution are becoming increasingly limited.

The governing circles of other First World nations seem to understand that unrestricted immigration would only exacerbate their domestic problems. During the 1990s, Britain, France, and Germany have moved to limit the immigrant influx into their respective nations. The attitude among governing circles in the U.S. is, however, dubious at best. In attempting to ascertain their stance, it is too simplistic to assume that conservatives favor immigration restriction while liberals oppose it. The fact is that both conservatives and liberals are subject to cross-pressures on the issue. People favoring immigration restriction may be found among both conservatives and liberals. It is an issue which cuts across ideological boundaries.

Conservatives who oppose immigration restriction do so for reasons quite other than those which move liberals into opposition. Generally, conservatives who favor unlimited immigration, a policy of "open borders," believe that any increase in population will be a stimulus to the economy of the nation. Liberals who oppose immigration restriction do so largely because they wish for the American population to be not more numerous but more diverse. One favors an increase in the quantity of people in the U.S., while the other favors a change in the quality of its people. Although spokesmen for these two points of view do not represent the rank and file of Americans who vote for either conservative or liberal candidates, since most Americans do not cast their ballots on an ideological basis, these ideologues are quite influential among the nation's governing elite.

The beliefs that there are almost no limits to growth, that population increases are a positive stimulus to the economy, and that the United States has a virtually unlimited capacity to assimilate masses of immigrants from the Third World are beliefs held by many prominent neoconservatives. The belief in virtually unlimited growth is particularly associated with such spokesmen as the late Herman Kahn, Julian Simon, Ben Wattenberg, and the editorial staff of the *Wall Street Journal*. Lindsey Grant, an ecologist, calls their belief that there are no limits to growth "the cornucopian fallacy." It is almost as if the Utopian impulse, discredited with regard to socialism, had somehow recoiled upon itself and re-emerged as the neoconservative and libertarian faith in an unlimited free market which will automatically solve all problems.

Herman E. Daly, professor of economics at Louisiana State University, characterizes the economics of Julian Simon as "ultimate confusion." The "belief in unlimited growth," Daly maintains, "is not a reasonable view for a crowded continent in which one man's production is another man's pollution and someone else's depletion."[362] Simon's denial of "resource finitude" is grounded on the assumption that resources, being infinitely divisible, must be infinite in amount, "a replay of Zeno's paradox." Adding to the confusion is Simon's denial of entropy, a refusal to recognize that "No resource can be totally recycled," while "energy cannot be recycled at all (except by expending more energy than the amount recycled)."[363]

Also confused are Simon's assumptions that more population and a larger economy to sustain that population are always good. More population does not translate into more prosperity because "even if everyone produces more than he consumes, it simply does not follow that more people will raise *per capita* production."[364] Similarly, a larger economy is not always a better economy because one must consider

> the physical scale of the economy relative to the overall ecosystem. The economy, guided by a competitive market, theoretically will attain a Pareto-optimum allocation of resources (a condition in which no one can be made better off without someone being made worse off). That is the best we can hope for from the market. But optimum allocation of resources within the economy is one thing, and optimum physical scale of the economy relative to ecosystem is something else. Nothing in the market system guarantees the latter. The scale of population and *per capita* resource use can be doubled or halved and the market will still find an optimal allocation. The inherent growth bias of the market, especially as supplemented by Keynesian policies, will push us beyond optimal sustainable scale. But the market will keep on optimally allocating resources. The market will always be making the best of an increasingly bad situation.[365]

Francis Fukuyama is another typical spokesman for the neoconservative position which welcomes "open borders" and population growth through immigration. In his "Immigrants and Family Values," published in the May, 1993, issue of *Commentary,* he denies the contention of traditional conservatives that Third World immigrants have values which inhibit their assimilation. Fukuyama does, however, admit to "three areas of particular concern" regarding the influx of immigrants. These areas include "the regional concentration of Hispanic immigration," "bilingualism and the elite Hispanic groups which promote and exist off it," and

> the effects of immigration on income distribution, particularly at the low end of the scale. The growing inequality of American income distribution . . . proceeds from the globalization of the American economy: low-skill labor increasingly has to compete with low-skill labor in Malaysia, Brazil, Mexico, and elsewhere. But it has also had to compete with low-skill immigrant labor coming into the country from the third world, which explains why Hispanics themselves tend to oppose further Hispanic immigration. The country as a whole may be better off economically as a result of this immigration, but those against whom immigrants directly compete have been hurt, just as they will be

hurt by the North American Free Trade Agreement (NAFTA), the General Agreement on Tariffs and Trade (GATT), and other trade-liberalizing measures that are good for the country as a whole.[366]

These three areas of concern would seem to be significant, but it is evident that Fukuyama and other neoconservatives believe that their impact will be negligible compared with the overall good to the country as a whole. Yet, what basis is there for that assumption? Will it not take decades to assess the relative impacts for good and ill? After that period, moreover, if the result proves to be other than that which was anticipated, how will it be possible to undo the damage?

It is evident that neoconservatives consider these to be unimportant questions. They think in terms of what it may be profitable to do in the next five years; that is what the catch phrase "good for the country as a whole" really means. Meanwhile, they ask the working people of America to take a leap of faith, a leap into the darkness, promising them that the firm ground of a better future will await them. Not even the latter promise, however, is to be extended to the unskilled, who in the United States, the land of their birth, the land of their forefathers, are to have no better way of life than that known by people in the failed societies of the Third World. The unskilled, moreover, are a rather larger group than one might at first suppose. Most people who are forced to find new employment, after finding no employment in the field in which they are skilled, find that they are unskilled in relation to other fields. The hope of the neoconservatives, obviously, is that the immiseration of those who are to be the newly unskilled and newly poor will be so gradual that they will not rise up in revolt.

Some conservatives have been misled by a positive stereotype of immigrants which is as inaccurate as are many of the negative stereotypes. Bemused by visions of Korean storekeepers, Chinese computer geniuses, and upwardly mobile Vietnamese surgeons, these conservatives believe that the newcomers will inject new energies into entrepreneurship and promote an appreciation of capitalism which is no longer to be found among many American citizens or even European immigrants. Jeane Kirkpatrick, for example, argues that "Only those who do not understand America believe that families that have been here for 10 generations are more American than the tens of thousands of new citizens naturalized last year."[367] Tom Bethell, also referring to Third World immigrant entrepreneurs, welcomes them "because they are the ones who will appreciate the country, will defend it and perpetuate it. University-educated Europeans are now of dubious value, if you ask me. They are inclined to think that America would be fine if only it were more like Europe. Which is exactly what we *don't* want."[368]

Kirkpatrick, Bethell, and others seem to be unaware of the fact that the success of Third World immigrant entrepreneurs is frequently generated by their employment of illegal aliens, child labor, and federal contracts awarded as "set-asides" to minority-owned businesses. The suggestion that Americans who lack the mysterious sources of capital available to Third World immigrant entrepreneurs and who, consequently, work for their livings as employees are, for that reason, somehow less worthy of respect as Americans is indeed strange. By this criterion, Simon Kenton, Daniel Boone, George Rogers Clark and other pioneers who died almost destitute were un-American. Even more strange, and repugnant, is the suggestion advanced by some enthusiasts for *laissez-faire* that aliens should be able to buy American citizenship by investing a specified amount of money in the country. Some conservatives with their praise of unrestrained capitalism almost seem to be determined to prove that what their worst enemies say about them is true.

Liberal opposition to immigration restriction is largely motivated by the movement which represents itself as "multiculturalism." Exponents of multiculturalism maintain with dogmatic vehemence that all cultures are equal, and that the United States must accept its destiny as a universal nation, a world nation, in which no one culture, and certainly not European culture, will be dominant. The ideal of multiculturalism is a nation which has no core culture, no ethnic core, no center other than a powerful state apparatus. Multiculturalism has become almost an official dogma in the mass media and in academe, two realms where the slightest expression of skepticism about its tenets is regarded as a kind of lese majesty.

The triumph of multiculturalism and the complete routing of any assumption that the United States should retain its basically European heritage has taken place in a single generation. For evidence of this, one need only read the record of the hearings which were held in the U.S. Senate early in 1965 regarding proposed legislation to abolish the national origins system of 1924, legislation which was enacted as the Immigration Reform Act of 1965. When Senator Sam Ervin of North Carolina expressed his concern that the U.S. might lose its cultural identity as a result of the proposed reform, he was assured by Senator Robert Kennedy that there was no basis for "any fears that this bill will change the ethnic, political, or economic make-up of the United States." Speaking in a similar vein, Senator Hiram Fong of Hawaii asserted that "I just want to make this point because the argument that the cultural pattern of the U.S. will change needs to be answered. Our cultural pattern will never be changed as far as America is concerned . . . . It will become more cosmopolitan but still there is that fundamental adherence to European culture."[369]

In the 1990s, only one generation after Senator Ervin expressed his concern about the nation's future ethnic composition, virtually no liberals in elected office would give utterance to such concerns. Indeed, few or no conservatives would dare to say what Ervin said. What happened in the interim to bring about such a remarkable transformation regarding what is acceptable in discussions of public policy? A likely explanation is that the activists of the New Left, who were most prominent during the period from 1965 to 1975, did not totally disappear, but transformed themselves into a significant portion of the liberal leadership of the succeeding generation.[370] In so doing, they seem to have given up most of their former radical beliefs, especially their opposition to capitalism, while retaining their commitment to a fundamental attack upon Western culture and those who embody it. The reasons why they retained this particular item on their agenda are doubtless complex, and not immediately pertinent to the immigration problem. Suffice it to be noted that the New Left's attack on the "Eurocentrism" of American culture has been either whole-heartedly adopted or at least quietly accepted by the mainstream of American liberalism.

Multiculturalism is even more entrenched as a dogma in the republic of letters than it is in the republic of politicians. Edward Abbey discovered this when he was invited by *The New York Times* to contribute an essay on "Immigration and Liberal Taboos." Months after he had submitted the essay, the newspaper informed him that it could not be printed due to "lack of space." Abbey, a prominent novelist and environmentalist, then submitted his essay to several different magazines, all of which had been eager to publish his work in the past. In turn, the essay was rejected by *Harper's, The Atlantic, The New Republic, Rolling Stone, Newsweek,* and *Mother Jones,* before being accepted by a minor regional weekly, whose editor insisted on publishing it with a refutation.

Abbey found himself catapulted out of the ranks of the politically correct and almost placed under a cultural taboo. The rejection of his essay undoubtedly resulted from its unambiguous challenge to multiculturalism. Arguing that "perhaps ever-continuing industrial and population growth is *not* the true road to human happiness," Abbey concluded that

> it might be wise for us as American citizens to consider calling a halt to the mass influx of even more millions of hungry, ignorant, unskilled, and culturally-morally-genetically impoverished people . . . . Especially when these uninvited millions bring with them an alien mode of life which -- let us be honest about this -- is not appealing to the majority of Americans. Why not? Because we prefer democratic government for one thing; because we still hope for an open, spacious, uncrowded, and beautiful -- yes, beautiful! -- society, for another. The alternative in the squalor, cruelty, and corruption of Latin America, is plain for all to see . . . . How many of us, truthfully, would *prefer* to be submerged in the Caribbean-Latin version of civilization? . . . Harsh words; but somebody has to say them.[371]

Abbey reveals the ultimate objective of the radical multiculturalists, which is not a state of peaceful co-existence among separate but equal cultures in a new "world nation," but rather the displacement of European American culture by one or more other cultures. After the transformation of America which they advocate has been effected, American civilization will no longer have its formerly European character. American civilization will have been effectively abolished. The Caribbean, however, will still be Caribbean in its culture and people; Mexico will remain Mexican; Japan will be as Japanese as ever, and so forth through the ranks of all of the other nations outside the European-Western world. They will be unscathed, or even strengthened, by the demise of the old European America. After all is said and done, it will have been only European Americans who will have lost their cultural identity, their political institutions, their traditional standard of living, and much else.

A great campaign has been waged in the political arena, in the mass media, in educational institutions and elsewhere to convince European Americans that their displacement from their central position in the nation's culture will be the justified outcome of inevitable changes or even, perhaps, a condign punishment. Advocates of the latter ascribe to the European American population a debt of historic guilt, accrued at some unstated point in time and having no statute of limitations, a debt which they collectively owe to other population groups because of the depredations of their forefathers against those groups. It is further argued that whatever disabilities other groups suffer are due to the sufferings of their ancestors. This argument, the ultimate rationale for the destruction of Eurocentric America, would have everyone believe that either the harm or the liability for ancestral grievances can be transmitted to descendants, a kind of theory of the inheritance of acquired characteristics which might be called Social Lamarckianism.

The European American elite held fast to the dogma of individual responsibility, inherited from the age of John Locke, during the several decades when the left was campaigning for its replacement by the Marxian dogma of Social Lamarckianism. During the 1970s, however, when the basic goal of public policy shifted from equal opportunity for individuals to equal outcomes for groups, the European American elite finally began to acquiesce in the new dogma. It was seen as the great compromise which had to be made to assure the continuing acceptance of consociational democracy by the other elites. Since the new dogma specifically attacks the legitimacy of the European role in American history, it is obvious that members of the European American elite, seeking to preserve the relative peace that prevails under consociational democracy, can only regard with trepidation anyone who would dare to question it. This horror arises not from any real faith in the new dogma on the part of the European American elite, a fact recognized by the elites of other groups, but from the prospect of the destabilization which might ensue.

Almost all of the opposition to a proposed curtailment of immigration arises, then, from these two fundamental interests: (1) the neoconservatives' interest in supporting corporate capitalism, regardless of the welfare of small businessmen and employees, by providing for it a supply of cheap labor, and (2) the left's interest in destroying the European basis of American civilization, a priority which rises above (or perhaps has even displaced) its long-trumpeted goal of destroying corporate capitalism.

The specific objections raised by this opposition are mostly either logically fallacious or patently absurd. To the latter category belongs the objection that the United States cannot control immigration because it is physically impossible to patrol its borders. This absurdity has been poignantly exposed by George F. Kennan, the noted artificer of America's successful policy of containing Communism, an authority in foreign affairs and military strategy who has few equals. Writing in 1993 in his memoir, *Around the Cragged Hill*, Kennan expresses dismay that the American political establishment, "while not loath to putting half a million armed troops into the Middle East to expel the armed Iraqis from Kuwait, confesses itself unable to defend its own southwestern border from illegal immigration by large numbers of people armed with nothing more formidable than a strong desire to get across it.'[372]

The example of a world power deploying hundreds of thousands of its troops throughout the world, yet neglecting to guard its own border against an alien invasion would seem to be without parallel. It does bear many points of similarity, however, to the decision of the rulers of the Roman Empire, late in the fourth century A.D., to allow a million Goths to cross the Danube and settle within its boundaries. Troops needed to patrol the Danube were stationed in Britain and other distant outposts. This development is considered by Edward Gibbon, the historian, to be "the principal and immediate cause of the fall of the Western empire of Rome.'[373] Gibbon notes that the Romans who favored an acceptance of the influx argued that the posterity of the Goths "would insensibly blend with the great body of the Roman people," an expectation which proved to be catastrophically inaccurate.[374]

Also patently absurd are the emotional objections to immigration restriction. It is argued, for example, that good Christians cannot close their nation to others, especially to those in need, that the United States has a destiny to act as an eleemosynary agent open to the whole world. This religiously tinged objection has been searchingly analyzed by Garrett Hardin, a biologist and ecologist. Hardin observes that the brother to whom Cain refers in his famous rhetorical question, "Am I my brother's keeper?" is but one brother, Cain's brother, not all brothers of everyone. Quantity is an all-important consideration. The U.S. simply cannot physically afford to open its borders to all of the wretched and poor who would inundate the country if it were to become an almsgiver to the world.[375]

Nothing in the scriptures of either Judaism or Christianity suggests that the existence of nations is contrary to the will of God. The Old Testament is largely the history of one exceptional nation, Israel, chosen to be an instrument of God's will. In the Mosaic books, God repeatedly commands Israel to stay separate from other nations. Israel defies the will of God when it accepts the "mixed multitude" (Exodus 12:38; Numbers 11:4) and when it takes "strange wives" (Ezra 10). Even in the New Testament, written in Greek during an age when the Stoics within the Roman Empire were teaching their concept of world citizenship, the nation *(ethnos)* is cited as a matter of fact, not of sin. The "Babylon" denounced in Revelation is not a real nation, but the Roman Empire, an early experiment in enforced multiculturalism. Acts 17:26 does affirm that God "hath made of one blood all nations of men," but also that he "hath determined. . . the bounds of their habitation."

Although the objections to immigration control are easily refuted, the opposition to immigration control is not as easily overcome. The opponents of immigration control, mostly neoconservatives and the New Left, represent only a small percentage of the American people, but they have an influence out of all proportion to their numbers. Further complicating the situation is the fact that the average American citizen, who favors immigration control, is relatively inactive as a citizen. Preoccupied with his work and other personal concerns, the average person does not effectively communicate to his legislators his thoughts regarding immigration and other issues. This lack of activity as a citizen is not evidence of apathy, but largely due to the average citizen's lack of free time and disposable income.

Assuming that there is not an unprecedented political uprising by American citizens, the prospects for the implementation of immigration control before the end of the century do not seem to be good. Genuine immigration control would involve effective patrols of the border and reduction of the annual influx of immigrants to 200,000 at the most. If such control is not attained, and immigrants, legal and illegal, continue to pour into the country as they have during the 1990s, then what is the outlook for America?

It would be a mistake to assume that a striking and catastrophic change will be immediately apparent. Change, rather, will be gradual, but no less constant, steady, irreversible, and ultimately ruinous to the American republic. The overall drift will be towards the extinction of European civilization in large areas of America, first at a slow but steady rate, but then at a rate steadily accelerating. Since immigrants will become citizens and, in turn, lobby and campaign (and demonstrate and threaten) for the admission of more of their kind, it is likely that at some future point the total annual influx will begin to rise. There is no real, physical reason why the United States cannot be occupied by 500 million people or more by the year 2050, rather than the almost 400 million predicted by the U.S. Census Bureau. Literally hundreds of millions of people in the Third World would come to America if they could. The more that immigrants are admitted to the U.S., just so much greater grow the political pressures to admit more immigrants.

Assuming a continuation of the levels of immigration attained during the early 1990s and no further acceleration of the immigrant influx, it is likely that the European American elite will attempt to keep consociational democracy operational by continuing to apply policies previously developed. The latter will soon, however, have to be supplemented with new concessions and adjustments to keep the elites of other groups more or less acquiescent. Affirmative action, "set-asides" for minority-owned businesses, and affirmative gerrymandering will be pursued as relentlessly as ever and, perhaps, supplemented with systems of weighted voting and multiple voting so that minorities may win greater representation in elective offices. Legislation against "hate crimes" may be supplemented by legislation against "hate speech." This might seem to be a great departure from the American political tradition. So it will be, but no greater than the earlier, and almost universally accepted, leap from equal opportunity for individuals to equal outcomes for groups.

One or two decades into the new century, the gradual economic immiseration of the lower two-thirds of the population, regardless of their citizenship or identity, will be evident and given various explanations, depending on the interests of those who hope to gain politically by offering explanations. There will be a growing European American underclass, which will be the object of some anxiety on the part of the European American elite. The elite's fear will be that one segment of the new European American underclass will, uniting with the masses of other groups, support the expropriation of the capital of all elites. Concurrent with this fear will be the contrary vision of a European American underclass, led by demagogues, and engaged in violent conflict with the masses of other groups. To a limited extent, there will be grounds for both fears, both of which will become growing realities.

The growing cultural dispossession of the European American population -- below the level of the elite, which will resort to private schools, private neighborhoods, and other private institutions, such as the walled, gated, and guarded communities which became increasingly common during the 1990s -- will also become more evident. The political subjugation of European Americans will become a reality in certain limited areas of the country, mostly in the Southwest and the Southeast. In these areas, European Americans will no longer be able to elect officials above the local level and will be forced to cast their votes for those non-Europeans whom they believe to be most sensitive to their concerns.

By the middle of the twenty-first century, again assuming a continuation of levels of immigration current during the 1990s, the country will have a much larger underclass of all origins and in almost all areas. European Americans in the Southwest and the Southeast quarters of the U.S. will be facing the imminent prospect of political subjugation following upon their economic immiseration and their cultural dispossession. Some European Americans will strike out violently and futilely. More of them will move to other sections of the U.S., especially the northern states. Some members of the European American elite will move to a prospering Europe or elsewhere and will attempt to continue their ownership of businesses in the U.S. Their U.S. properties eventually will be expropriated.

By the latter half of the twenty-first century, the cultural dispossession of which Edward Abbey warned will be a reality, but a reality rather more complex than the one he describes. Rather than a total displacement of European American culture by a Caribbean-Latin culture, as Abbey predicts, there will be a displacement of European culture in the southern half of the U.S. In the Southwest quarter and along the Pacific coast, Hispanic culture will uneasily co-exist with Asian culture and the "Anglo" remnants. In the Southeast quarter, there will be an Afro-Caribbean dominance with a larger "Anglo" remnant and some Hispanic enclaves.

This cultural-political configuration will not itself be permanent and will be productive of further inter-group conflict, much of which will be translated into regional conflict. The northern third of the U.S. will remain overwhelmingly European, largely Germanic (Dutch, German, Scandinavian) in the Midwest and with a mix of all European groups, but predominantly Irish and Mediterranean, in the extreme Northeast. Americans of British origin will be scattered in diminishing numbers throughout the country, with most of them located in the upper South, Border States, and lower Midwest.[376] European Americans in these areas will still elect European American officials and will be voting as conscious Europeans. They will be increasingly unhappy that they contribute more federal revenues than are returned to them. Their state of political alienation from the remainder of the country will resemble that of Northern Californians and Southern Brazilians in the 1990s.[377]

Even in areas dominated by European Americans, however, there will be urban enclaves of non-Europeans. The ethnic map will be a Balkanized mosaic with regional strongholds for major groups. The result will be a melange of peoples, an America without Americans, which will be governable only through the adoption of the separatist mechanisms developed in Canada, Switzerland, and Belgium. Only if these mechanisms are put into operation early will it be possible to avoid the chronic violent conflict that has historically been characteristic of the Balkans. It is very doubtful, however, that the elites of the various groups will possess the foresight and flexibility to act in time to allow a peaceful "Swiss" solution and, thereby, avoid a violent "Bosnian" solution. Elites of the contending groups will strive first of all to include as much territory as possible in the areas where they will be recognized as having *imperium in imperio*.

Many writers have predicted that the decline and fall of the American republic will be followed by a period of Caesarism analogous to that of the Roman Empire.[378] The analogy is flawed, however, because that empire, although multicultural and multinational, nonetheless was almost exclusively populated by members of one human subspecies. An American empire, a forced structure of power imposed upon geographically separated, culturally distinct, and highly visible population blocs, could endure for only a brief period before toppling into the remnants of peoples which composed it. If America follows the example of Rome, it will have a Rienzi, or perhaps only a Porcaro, but no Caesars.

Such a sad denouement to the American story seems preposterous, impossible, beyond belief, but only because it confounds all the expectations for the future which people have been conditioned to entertain by past experiences. The assumption of a linear historical development, a kind of teleological mechanism working within history which ensures the gradual advancement of all mankind, has been questioned by many professional historians all during the twentieth century. In the popular consciousness, however, it has fallen to the ground only with the Berlin Wall, the first in a series of events in which that which was expected to endure for all of the foreseeable future began to collapse into ruins. A world which had anticipated the triumph of socialism and cosmopolitanism has, instead, found itself, in the words of the historian John Lukacs, ''near the end of the so-called Modern Age,'' and threatened by ''two dangerous circumstances . . . . One is the thrust for increasing wealth; the other, for tribal power.''[379] It is these two circumstances which particularly menace the American nation.

Why should an American living in 1995 or in 2000 care about the America of 2030 or of 2050?

The reason why he should care is two-fold. First, the America of the future is already stirring in the present, only on a smaller and limited scale, only in particular areas of the country. Secondly, this entering wedge of the future does not have behind it any thrust of historical inevitability. Historical inevitability is, in fact, the greatest of the mistaken assumptions of the past which have fallen to the ground with the great changes in Europe.

In other terms, the average American should care because he already may be suffering from the first intimations of such an adverse future and because he can definitely do something to avert and even reverse its onward course. Stoic acceptance is an appropriate stance only for the defeated subjects of an empire.

Looking at the one bright corner in an otherwise gloomy scene, one can hope that the collapse of old assumptions and expectations may yet give the

American people a fighting chance to win for themselves and their posterity a new vision and reality of nationhood that will be greater than any which they have theretofore known.

# Notes

1. Richard D. Lamm and Gary Imhoff, *The Immigration Time Bomb: The Fragmenting of America* (New York: E.P. Dutton, 1985), p. 99.

2. *Up 'Til Now: A Memoir* (San Diego: Harcourt Brace Jovanovich, 1987), p. 246. See also Senator McCarthy's *A Colony of the World: The United States Today* (New York: Hippocrene Books, 1992).

3. "The Future of North America," *The Futurist*, Aug. 1980, p. 22.

4. "Race in America," in *Tocqueville's America 1982* (Washington, D.C.: LTV Corp., 1982), p. 91.
Gore Vidal, writing in his *At Home: Essays 1982-1988* (New York: Random House, 1988), has presented the same idea, in his characteristic style, as follows:

> These two clumsy empires, the Soviet Union and the United States are now becoming unstuck. Only by force can the Soviets control their Armenians and Moslems and Mongols, and only by force can we try to control a whole series of escalating race wars here at home, as well as the brisk occupation of the southern tier of the United States by those Hispanics from whom we stole land in 1847 (p. 302).

Theodore H. White, in his *America in Search of Itself* (New York: Harper & Row, 1982), warned as follows of the growth of linguistic separatism:

> Some Hispanics have, however, made a demand never voiced by immigrants before that the United States, in effect, officially recognize itself as a bicultural, bilingual nation. Puerto Rico, a 'commonwealth' within the Union, is Spanish-speaking . . . . The Hispanics demand that the United States become a bilingual country, with all children entitled to be taught in the language of their heritage, at public expense . . . . Bilingualism is an awkward word -- but it has torn apart communities from Canada to Brittany, from Belgium to India (p. 367).

119

Several other spokesmen for the tradition of New Deal liberalism have either openly favored immigration restriction or have recognized the turbulence engendered in a nation when it becomes simply another multi-ethnic state. George F. Kennan, the artificer of America's successful foreign policy of the containment of Communism, took a stance in favor of immigration restriction in his *Around the Cragged Hill* (New York: W.W. Norton, 1993). While not openly favoring immigration restriction, Arthur M. Schlesinger, Jr., in his *The Disuniting of America* (New York: W.W. Norton, 1992), and Senator Daniel P. Moynihan, in his *Pandaemonium: Ethnicity in International Politics* (New York: Oxford Univ. Pr., 1993), have recognized the problems confronted by liberal democracy in a multi-ethnic state when assimilation fails.

5. (Alexandria, Va.: The Center for Immigration Research and Education, 1982), p. 17.

6. Bouvier and Davis, pp. 21-22.

7. See the appendix to M.E. Bradford, *Sentiment or Survival: Crisis in the Immigration Policy of the United States* (Monterey, Va.: American Immigration Control Foundation, 1984), pp. 14-15. The projections in this appendix were prepared by demographer Davis subsequent to the publication of *Immigration and the Future Racial Composition of the United States*.

8. *Ibid.*

9. Celia W. Dugger, "Latin Influx, Crime Prompt Flight North," *The Miami Herald*, 3 May 1987, Sec. B, p. 1.

10. Dugger, Sec. B, p. 2.

11. See Richard Wallace, "S. Florida Grows to a Latin Beat," *The Miami Herald*, 8 Mar. 1991, Sec. A, p. 1.

12. Thomas Muller, *The Fourth Wave: California's Newest Immigrants* (Washington, D.C.: The Urban Institute Press, 1984), p. 17.

13. Muller, p. 18.

14. Ellis E. Conklin, "The New Ellis Island," *Indianapolis Star*, 23 Feb. 1986, Sec. F, p. 1.

15. "Los Angeles Dream is Dying for Some, Thriving for Others," *The New York Times*, 28 Aug. 1989, p. 1.

16. *op. cit.*, p. 9. See also Elizabeth Fernandez, "California Dreamers: A Rude Awakening," *San Francisco Examiner*, 30 July 1989, Sec. A, p. 1, which reports

that "lurking beneath the decision of some who move is a generalized impression that the state backslid because it was saturated by 'foreigners'" (p. 14).

In 1987, James Johnson, a geographer at the University of Southern California, reported evidence of "black flight" from Los Angeles. According to "Black Flight to the South," *Society,* July-Aug. 1987, p. 2, "In cities experiencing a rapid influx of Latino and Asian immigrants, such as Los Angeles, Johnson believes other factors may be contributing to black flight. 'In South Central Los Angeles, where 90 percent of the black population of metropolitan Los Angeles lives, resources are already scarce,' says Johnson. 'As Latinos move into formerly all-black enclaves, competition grows for housing, jobs, and public services -- and so does the potential for black/brown conflict.'" See also Scott Armstrong, "Los Angeles Faces Black Exodus," *The Christian Science Monitor,* 13 Aug. 1990, p. 6.

17. "L.A.'s Atlantic Boulevard: Ethnic Slice of the Future," *Washington Post,* 19 Jan. 1988, Sec. A, p. 3. According to Kevin Roderick, "The Quality of L.A. Life," *Los Angeles Times Magazine,* 2 Apr. 1989, p. 9, "Nearly half of Los Angeles residents say they have considered moving away in the past year." See also Paul Nussbaum, "A Not-Too-Fond Farewell to L.A.," *Philadelphia Inquirer,* 6 August 1989, Sec. A, p. 1; Lew Lord and Peter Dworkin, "California's Other Bedeviling Problems," 30 Oct. 1989, p. 36.

18. Ed. Nathan Glazer, (San Francisco: Institute for Contemporary Studies, 1985), p. 131.

19. p. 10. The following observation by Bruno challenges the ready assumption of some conservatives that native workers voluntarily vacate fields of employment taken over by aliens: "I have been asked why you don't see more American field workers. Some of the Mexican workers have been heard to comment that it is because the white American male is lazy, that he won't do this type of work. For one thing, most labor contractors are Hispanic and hire accordingly. Citizens and legal aliens are being replaced by the imported aliens" (p. 11).

David Freed, "The 'Bricks': Big Profit in Slum Decay," *Los Angeles Times,* 30 July 1989, Sec. I, pp. 1, 30, mentions the role of the new immigrants, as both renters and landlords, in the generation of the new slums of Los Angeles.

See Timothy Egan, "Dream Gone Sour: Pollution and High Costs," *The New York Times,* 29 Dec. 1991, p. 20, for an account of an "Anglo" family's experience of downward economic mobility in Southern California, followed by their recovery of a higher standard of living through their move to Washington state.

20. Teresa Watanabe, "Population Explosion Hits California," *San Jose Mercury News,* 5 Feb. 1987, Sec. A, p. 16. According to "Births to Hispanics Are Increasing in the U.S.," *Wall Street Journal,* 16 Aug. 1988, p. 25, "Hispanic births accounted for 17% of all births in 1985, the most recent year data are available. Forty percent of Hispanic births were in California and 25% in Texas." According to these statistics, compiled by the National Center for Health Statistics, a large majority of all births in California in 1985 were births to Hispanics, mostly of Mexican origin.

21. Jay Mathews, "Anglos May Become Minority in California Schools," *Washington Post,* 21 Aug. 1988, Sec. A, p. 4.

22. "Whites Lose Majority Role in State's Schools," *The [San Diego] Tribune,* 7 Sept. 1988, Sec. A, p. 3. According to Cynthia Patrick, "Report Predicts Tough Future for State's Children," *The Stanford University Campus Report,* 15 February 1989, p. 7, "Currently, minorities make up more than half of California's school population. The fastest growing of these minorities are Hispanics and Asians. By the year 2000, 42 percent of California's children will be white, 36 percent will be Hispanic, 13 percent Asian and 9 percent black. At present, one out of four California schoolchildren speaks a language other than English at home."

23. "Hispanic Numbers Up by 1/3," *The [Corpus Christi] Caller Times,* 7 Sept. 1988, Sec. A, p. 1.

24. *The World Almanac and Book of Facts: 1989* (New York: World Almanac, 1988), pp. 538-539.

25. Maria Halkias, "Hispanic Impact on Texas Growing," *Dallas Morning News,* 19 Dec. 1986, Sec. D, p. 2.

26. "Hispanic Power," *Houston Post,* 1 Mar. 1987. Editorial page.

27. Matt Moffett, "Attention to Area's Demographic Change Makes Houston's Fiesta Stores a Success," *The Wall Street Journal,* 23 Oct. 1986, p. 35.

28. "Hispanic Power," *loc. cit.*

29. Steve Olafson, Guy Cantwell, and Grace Lim, "The Changing Face of Houston," *Houston Post,* circa 1986.

30. Halkias, Sec. D, p. 2.

31. Maria Halkias, "The Changing Face of Texas," *Dallas Morning News,* 19 Dec. 1986, Sec. A, p. 24.

32. Paul Recer, "Hispanics Changing Face of Texas," *The Monitor,* [McAllen, Texas], 24 May 1987, Sec. A, p. 1. According to Lorwen Connie Harris in her *Children, Choices, and Change: An Adaptation of the Darker Side of Childhood* (Austin: Hogg Foundation for Mental Health, University of Texas, 1988), "By some estimates, Hispanics will represent 36 percent of the Texas population by the year 2000 and 54 percent of the population by 2025" (p. 18).

33. Joel Williams, "Central Americans Flood South Texas," *The Monitor,* [McAllen, Texas], 20 Nov. 1988, Sec. A, p. 1.

34. "Debate on Sanctuary Bill Expected," *FAIR Immigration Report*, Feb. 1988, p. 2.

35. Jacob V. Lamar, "The Immigration Mess: A Surge of Central American Refugees Finds the U.S. Unprepared," *Time*, 27 Feb. 1989, p. 14.

36. Sol Sanders, "The Coming Troubles," *Orbis: A Journal of World Affairs*, 32 (Winter 1988): 55.

37. U.S. Department of Justice, Immigration and Naturalization Service, *Commissioner's Communique: Keeping You Informed*, May/June 1988, p. 1.

38. "Illegal Alien Amnesty Applicants Just the Tip of the Iceberg," *FAIR Immigration Report*, July 1988, p. 1. Evelyn Hsu, *Washington Post*, 19 Mar. 1988, Sec. B, p. 5, reports that many illegal immigrants who are not even eligible for amnesty apply nonetheless in order to receive temporary work permits.

39. *Wall Street Journal*, 6 Nov. 1987, pp. 1, 11.

40. "New Law Fails to Stem Flow of Aliens," *San Francisco Examiner*, 1 May 1988, Sec. A, p. 1. Ross quotes Jorge Bustamente, an immigration researcher, as saying that "Immigration obeys the law of supply and demand, not the laws of immigration." Dugger, Sec. B, p. 2.

41. Patrick McDonnell, "Immigration Law Failing, Study Finds," *Los Angeles Times*, 9 June 1989, Sec. I, p. 1. See also Sandy Lejeune, "Immigration Reform Has Already Flopped," *Los Angeles Herald Examiner*, 11 May 1989, Sec. A, p. 15; "Experts Question Results of Illegal-Alien Legislation," *[Ft. Lauderdale] Sun-Sentinel*, 18 June 1989, Sec. A, p. 14. Pauline Yoshihashi, "Employer Sanctions and Illegal Workers," *The Wall Street Journal*, 26 May 1989, Sec. B, p. 1, also focuses on the situation in California.

42. Tim Golden, "Mexicans Head North Despite Rules on Jobs," *The New York Times*, 13 Dec. 1991, Sec. A, p. 20. For the impact of false documentation, see Robert Suro, "Traffic in Fake Documents Is Blamed As Illegal Immigration Rises Anew," *The New York Times*, 26 Nov. 1990, Sec. A, p. 9.

43. *Annals of the American Academy of Political and Social Science*, 485 (May 1986): 23-33.

44. (Washington, D.C.: Center for Immigration Studies, 1986), p. 11.

45. *Ibid.*, p. 24.

46. *Ibid.*, p. 32. See also Population Reference Bureau's "Mexico's Population: A Profile," *Population Education Interchange*, May 1987.

47. "Mexican Immigration: Spectre of a Fortress America?" *Strategic Review,* Winter 1986, pp. 30-38. See also Sol Sanders, *Mexico: Chaos on Our Doorstep,* (New York: Macmillan, 1986).

48. As quoted in Bouvier and Simcox, p. 40.

49. Marjorie Miller, "Despite New Laws, U.S. Still a Lure in Mexico," *Los Angeles Times,* 21 Aug. 1989, Part I, p. 10.

50. *Ibid.,* Part I, p. 1.

51. *Ibid.,* Part I, p. 11.

52. (New York: Oxford Univ. Pr., 1964), p. 85.

53. *Ibid.*

54. *Ibid.*

55. *Annals of the American Academy of Political and Social Science,* 454 (Mar. 1981): 178-188.

56. *Ibid., p. 183.*

57. *Ibid.*

58. *Ibid.,* p. 185.

59. This has been most fully documented in the case of Asian American enterprises. See Edna Bonacich and John Modell, *The Economic Basis of Ethnic Solidarity: Small Business in the Japanese-American Community,* (Berkeley: Univ. of California Pr., 1980); and Ivan Light, "Asian Enterprise in America: Chinese, Japanese and Koreans in Small Business," in *Self-Help in Urban America,* ed. Scott Cummings, (New York: Kennikat, 1980), pp. 33-57. For numerous specific examples of the success enjoyed by the strategy of ethnic economic enclaves, see Eva Pomice, "The Ties That Bind -- And Enrich," *U.S. News & World Report,* 25 Apr. 1988, pp. 42-43, 46.
Ethnic separatism, with its concomitant sense of group solidarity, also may account for the fact that Hutterites and Amish, despite their frequent use of "outdated" farming methods, can prosper while "family farmers" go into bankruptcy. The same principle may account for the success of business enterprises owned by members of the Church of Jesus Christ of Latter-day Saints, the role of the Patels in hotel-keeping, and the predominance of Hasidic Jews in the trade of diamond-cutting.

60. Robert Pear, "Aliens Who Stay in Clusters Are Said to Do Better," *The New*

*York Times,* 11 Mar. 1982, Sec. A., p. 24. For more information on Portes' study, see Kenneth L. Wilson and Alejandro Portes, "Ethnic Enclaves: A Comparison of the Cuban and Black Economies in Miami," *American Journal of Sociology,* 88(2): 295-319.

61. Pear, *op cit.* See also Reynaldo Baca and Dexter Bryan, "The 'Assimilation' of Unauthorized Mexican Workers: Another Social Science Fiction?'', *Hispanic Journal of Behavioral Sciences,* 5(Mar. 1983): 1-20. The abstract of this report follows:

> 1,391 unauthorized Mexican-American workers living in Los Angeles were surveyed as to (1) social and demographic characteristics, (2) citizenship aspirations and residency rights preferences, (3) careers and occupational aspirations and (4) family resettlement plans. Results reveal a binational life-style. Rather than giving up ties to Mexico Ss worked in the U.S. and maintained residences in both countries. While an assimilationist perspective would suggest that extended residence would result in the acceptance of the values and practices of the US, the present study suggests an alternative hypothesis: Extended residence will result in an awareness of the limited opportunities for Mexicans in the US and an awareness of the advantages of living in both countries. Rather than study the assimilation of Mexican workers, it would be more fruitful to study the adaptation to living in 2 countries.

62. Randolph E. Schmid, "Most Immigrants Still Settle in Urban Areas, Survey Shows,'' *Washington Post,* 29 Aug. 1988, sec. A, p. 13.

63. George Vernez and David Ronfeldt, "The Current Situation in Mexican Immigration,'' *Science,* 8 Mar. 1991, p. 1190.

64. Sydney P. Freedberg and Luis Feldstein Soto, "Miami Splinters in Three Parts,'' *Miami Herald,* 13 Feb. 1989, Sec. B, p.1. Freedberg and Soto report the following percentages of the three ethnic groupings in Dade County: "Latins: 46 percent. Anglos: 34 percent. Blacks: 21 percent. (The percentages add up to 101 because about 1 percent of Dade residents are black Latins.)''

By the end of 1990, Miami's Puerto Ricans were protesting their exclusion from community affairs by the generally more affluent Cubans. See "Looking for a Place in the Sun,'' *Newsweek,* 17 Dec. 1990, p. 32. For accounts of the rising tensions between the black and the Cuban communities in Miami, see "In Miami, Rivalries of Minority Groups Fan Riot's Flames,'' *The Wall Street Journal,* 20 Jan. 1989, Sec. A, p. 1; Morris S. Thompson, "Behind the Trouble in Miami's Back Streets,'' *Washington Post,* 23 Jan. 1989, Sec. A, p. 1; Barry Bearak, "Miami Ponders Racial Unrest as Latino Impact Stirs Anger Among City's Blacks,'' *Los Angeles Times,* 20 Mar. 1989, Sec. I, p. 14; Jeanne DeQuine, "Racial Tensions Increasing in Miami,'' *Detroit News,* 8 July 1990, Sec. B, p. 4; and Laura Parker, "Miami, a City Intransigent: Blacks Boycott, Mayor Balks at Two Words,'' *Washington Post,* 20 Dec. 1990, Sec. A, p. 10.

Future ethnic divisions in southern California, with its large population of Asians, may prove to be even more complex than those in Miami.

65. (Cambridge Univ. Pr., 1979), p. 77.

66. "The Political Integration of Mexican American Children: A Generational Analysis," *International Migration Review*, 16 (Spring 1982): 173-174.

67. Yankelovich, Skelly & White, *Spanish U.S.A., 1984*, (New York: Yankelovich, Skelly & Wright, 1984), pp. 9-10.

68. "U.S. Hispanics Largely Staying in Own Culture," *San Diego Tribune*, 14 Apr. 1989, Sec. A, p. 28.

69. Seth Mydans, "They're in a New Home, But Feel Tied to the Old," *The New York Times*, 30 June 1991, Sec. A, p. 8.

70. *Ibid.*

71. "Advertisers Learn to Speak Spanish -- the Hard Way," *Television/Radio Age*, 25 July 1988, p. A4. The article explains that the discrepancy in numbers of stations is due to the exclusion of smaller stations from Arbitron surveys. According to "SRC Wins Again for Spanish Radio in Door-to-Door Surveys," *Television/Radio Age*, 2 May 1988, "The possibility exists that Arbitron and Birch underreport Spanish listening" (p. 49). Scott Brown, "Madison Avenue's Big Latin Beat," *Time*, 20 July 1987, refers without further elaboration to "nearly 600 full-time Spanish-language television and radio stations, hundreds of Hispanic newspapers and countless billboards and bus posters in Spanish-speaking neighborhoods."

72. *Ibid.*, p. A3. According to Eliot Tiegel, "KTLA(TV) Says It in Spanish: Pioneering With SAP Technology Has Its Surprises," *Television/Radio Age*, 19 Sept. 1988, pp. 49-50, bilingual broadcasting is the wave of the future. SAP or second audio programming permits simultaneous broadcasting in Spanish of English language programs to homes having stereophonic television receivers.

73. "Bright Prospects for Speaking Spanish," *Broadcasting*, 26 Sept. 1988, p. 54.

74. See Gordon, "Models of Pluralism: The New American Dilemma," pp. 186-187, on the significance of the abandonment of insistence on use of one language.

75. Tom Bethel, "Against Bilingual Education," *Harper's*, Feb. 1979, p. 30.

76. "'75 Voting Act -- Help for Those Who Don't Read English," *U.S. News & World Report*, 11 Aug. 1975, p. 28.

77. Linda Chavez, "Is Spanish Wrong Signal to Latinos?" *Los Angeles Times*, 8 Aug. 1988.

78. *Ibid.*

79. Such advertisements have, of course, also become increasingly apparent in the Southwest. For a speculation on the legal question this may raise, see John P. Kohl and David B. Stephens, "The Increasing Use of Bilingual Requirements in Classified Advertisements: A Questionable or Illegal Personnel Practice?" *Labor Law Journal,* 39 (May 1988): 307-311.

80. Robert H. Cordova, "Bilingual U.S. by Turn of the Century?" *Houston Chronicle,* 11 Mar. 1985, Sec. 1, p. 15.

81. Ricardo Chavira, "Assimilate? Extra Culture and Language Are Advantage," *The Monitor, [McAllen, Texas]* 5 July 1987, Sec. A, p. 18.

82. Jonathan Yardley, "'Eurocentrism' and Biases Just as Bad," *Washington Post,* 17 Apr. 1989, Sec. B, p. 2.

83. "California Babel: The City of the Future Is a Troubling Prospect If It's to Be Los Angeles," *The Wall Street Journal,* 12 June 1989, Sec. A, p. 6. See also Michael Meyer, "Los Angeles 2010: A Latino Subcontinent," *Time,* 9 Nov. 1992, pp. 32-33.

84. "City of Angels Evolving into a City of Contrasts," *Los Angeles Business Journal,* 20 May 1991, p. 1.

85. *Ibid.,* p. 12.

86. *Ibid.,* pp. 13-14.

87. "Do Immigrants Underpin L.A. Business World?" *Los Angeles Business Journal,* 27 May 1991, p. 1.

88. See Anthony DePalma, "Separate Ethnic Worlds Grow on Campus," *The New York Times,* 18 May 1991, p. 1.

89. *Ibid.,* p. 7.

90. Carl Irving, "UC-Berkeley's Face Changing," *San Francisco Examiner,* 20 Aug. 1989, Sec. A, p. 15.

91. See Elaine Woo and Kim Kowsky, "Schools' Racial Mix Boils Over," *Los Angeles Times,* 14 June 1991, Sec. A, p. 1. For further details concerning racial conflict in California's public schools, see Carol Ness, "Majority Turning Into a Minority," *San Francisco Chronicle,* 14 Apr. 1991, Sec. A, p. 1, and "Coping in Stockton," *The Economist,* 12 Oct. 1990, p. 9.

92. Seth Mydans, "As Cultures Meet, Gang War Paralyzes a City in California," *The New York Times,* 6 May 1991, Sec. A, p. 1.

93. See Jack Miles, "Blacks vs. Browns," *Atlantic Monthly,* Oct. 1992, pp. 41-5+. Miles quotes (on p. 45) the following editorial, which appeared in the May 15, 1992, issue of *La Prensa San Diego,* a Mexican American newspaper:

> Though confronted with catastrophic destruction of the Latino businesses, which were 60% of the businesses destroyed, major looting by Blacks and by the Central Americans living in the immediate area and a substantial number of Hispanics being killed, shot and/or injured, every major television station was riveted to the concept that the unfolding events could only be understood if viewed in the context of the Black and White experiences. They missed the crucial point: The riots were not carried out against Blacks or Whites, they were carried out against the Latino and Asian communities by the Blacks! . . .
> Faced with nearly a million and a half Latinos taking over the inner city, Blacks revolted, rioted and looted . . . . Not only are they in danger of losing influence, public offices, and control of the major civil rights mechanisms, they now see themselves being replaced in the pecking order by the Asian community, in this case the Koreans.

94. "No Se Habla Espanol," *Time,* 21 Nov. 1988, p. 86. See also "Say It in English," *Newsweek,* 20 Feb. 1989, pp. 22-23.

95. On the controversy in Miami, see George Volsky, "Approval of Antibilingual Measure Causes Confusion and Worry in Miami Area," *The New York Times,* 9 Nov. 1980, p. 24. See also, Celia W. Dugger, "Latin 'Non-Group' Helps Quash Bilingual Vote," *Miami Herald,* 6 Sept. 1987, Sec. B, p. 1. For the controversy in Texas, see Doralisa Pilarte, "English First Movement Seen Primarily as a Power Struggle," *Houston Chronicle,* 26 May 1987, Sec. 1, p.9.

96. "Southland Struggles to Cope With Immigrants and Their Languages," *Los Angeles Times,* 12 Mar. 1989, p. 18.

97. *Ibid.*

98. See Daniel B. Wood, "Monterey Park Seeks Harmony," *The Christian Science Monitor,* 18 Oct. 1990, p. 6. For the challenge confronting non-Asian merchants in Monterey Park, see "The Lesson of Monterey Park," *Inc.,* July 1987, p. 52.

99. Frank Viviano, "Californians Face New Ethnic Mosaic," *San Francisco Chronicle,* 24 July 1989.

100. "The Melting Pot Boils Over," *The Economist,* 13 Oct. 1990, p. 8.

101. "Bill to Make English Official Language Draws Outspoken Opposition," *Arkansas Gazette,* 15 Feb. 1987, Sec. C, p. 6.

102. See *Facts on File,* 9 Feb. 1990, p. 85.

103. Alfonso Chardy, "Should Puerto Rico Become a State? Controversy Likely if Referendum Held," *Arkansas Gazette,* 14 Feb. 1989, Sec. A, p. 3. See also Judith Havemann, "Vote on Puerto Rico's Status Backed," *The Washington Post,* 15 Nov. 1989, Sec. A. p.18. For President Bush's memorandum, see the *Federal Register,* 2 Dec. 1992, p. 57093.

104. Joel Garreau, *The Nine Nations of North America* (New York: Avon, 1982), p. 218.

105. "Official English or English Only," *English Journal,* 72 (Mar. 1988), 20. The National Council of Teachers of English has adopted a resolution condemning the "official English" movement. See "1986 NCTE Resolution on English as the 'Official Language,'" *English Journal,* 77 (Mar. 1988):17.

106. *Ibid.*

107. Felton West, "Hispanics Growing Fast in Texas," *Houston Post,* 26 Feb. 1989, Sec. C, p. 3.

108. "Southland Struggles to Cope With Immigrants and Their Languages," *loc. cit.*

109. Lori Silver, "Education Depart., in Shift, Favors Bilingual Education," *Los Angeles Times,* 26 Aug. 1989, Part I, p.1.

110. *Ibid.,* pp. 20, 1.

111. *The Nature of Prejudice.* Abridged ed. (Garden City, N.Y.: Doubleday Anchor Books, 1958), p. 131.

112. "Norwegian-American Attitudes Toward Assimilation During Four Periods of their History in America, 1825-1930," *Journal of Ethnic Studies,* 9(Spring 1981):62-3.

113. *The Ethnic Revival* (Cambridge: Cambridge Univ. Pr., 1981), pp. 15-7.

114. (New York: Crown, 1988), pp. 4-5.

115. See Blayne Cutler, "Welcome to the Borderlands," *American Demographics,* Feb. 1991, p. 47.

116. Cutler, p. 46.

117. *Ibid.*

118. "U.S. Personal Income," *Washington Post,* 26 May 1988, Sec. A, p. 19. For

a graphic account of poverty in the *colonias* of south Texas, see Paul Weingarten, "Third World -- deep in the heart of Texas: Squalor is rampant in makeshift 'towns'," *San Francisco Examiner*, 26 June 1988, Sec. A, p. 4.

119. For an overview of this program, see E.R. Stoddard, *Maquila: Assembly Plants in Northern Mexico* (El Paso, Tex.: Texas Western Pr., 1987).

120. *The New Realities: in Government and Politics, in Economics and Business, in Society and World View* (New York: Harper & Row, 1989), pp. 39-40.

121. *Ibid.*, p. 41.

122. Tim Golden, "Mexicans Head North Despite Rules on Jobs," *The New York Times*, 13 Dec. 1991, Sec. A, p. 20.

123. *Ibid.*

124. 43(2)(Winter 1990):383.

125. *Ibid.*

126. See Walter Russell Mead, *The Low-Wage Challenge to Global Growth* (Washington, D.C.: Economic Policy Institute, 1991).

127. See Steve L. Hawkins, "Tokyo Opens a Southern Trade Route," *U.S. News & World Report*, 3 Aug. 1987, pp. 40-1.

128. For a look at one unsavory aspect of the MexAmerican economic miracle, see Matt Moffett, "Working Children: Underage Laborers Fill Mexican Factories, Stir U.S. Trade Debate," *The Wall Street Journal*, 8 Apr. 1991, p. 1. Much has been published about possible adverse impacts on workers in the U.S. See, for example, Hobart Rowan, "Trade Fight at the Rio Grande," *The Washington Post*, 21 Feb. 1991, Sec. A, p. 21.

129. See Michael Smith, "The Aztlan Migrations of the Nahuatl Chronicles: Myth or History?" *Ethnohistory*, 31(1984):153-86.

130. In *Chicano Manifesto*, ed. Armando B. Renden. (New York: Collier Books, 1971), p. 336.

131. (San Francisco: Canfield Press, 1972), p. 7.

132. "Irredentism," in *Encyclopedia of the Social Sciences*, 1st ed. (1937; rpt. New York: Macmillan, 1950), VIII, 325.

133. *Ibid.*, VIII, 326.

134. (Notre Dame, Ind.: Univ. of Notre Dame Press, 1987), pp. 95-6.

135. "La guerra de Texas se remova: Mexican Insurrection and Carrancista Ambitions, 1900-1920," *Aztlan: International Journal of Chicano Studies Research*, 11(Spring 1980):16.

136. *Ibid.*, 11(Spring 1980):17.

137. *Ibid.*, 11(Spring 1980):19.

138. See Arthur Rosenberg, *Democracy and Socialism* (Boston: Beacon Press, 1965), p. 238.

139. See Donald J. Devine, "The Political Culture of the United States," *The New York Times Magazine*, 9 May 1982, p. 50.

140. Carlos Loret de Mola, "The Great Invasion: Mexico Recovers Its Own," *Excelsior*, 20 July 1982, Sec. A, p. 7.

141. "Majority of Mexicans in Poll View U.S. as 'Enemy'," *The Atlanta Constitution*, 26 Aug. 1986, Sec. A, p. 5.

142. "Just Forget the Alamo! Ponder Yankees' Sins," *The New York Times*, 7 Jan. 1988, p. 4.

143. See Gideon Kanner, "Whose Rights Are Being Trespassed Here?" *Los Angeles Times*, 22 Jan. 1990.

144. See Ron Roach, "Assembly Calls for Delay in Building Border Ditch," *San Diego Tribune*, 26 May 1989, Sec. A, p. 6.

145. See John C. Henry, "'Buy Texas,' Would Give Edge to Minorities," *Austin American-Statesman*, 31 May 1987, Sec. B, p.2.

146. See Debbie Graves, "Tuition Break OK'd for Mexican Citizens," *Austin American-Statesman*, 31 May 1987, Sec. B, p. 2.

147. Patrice Armstrong, "Cisneros: U.S. Must Look South," *Albuquerque Journal*, 1 Feb. 1986, Sec. B, p. 2.

148. See "Texas Lt. Governor Wants Open Borders," *Border Watch*, Mar. 1990, p. 4.

149. See Wilfredo Ramirez, "Babbitt: Halve Mexico Debt to U.S.," *[San Antonio] Express News*, 28 June 1987, Sec. C, p. 1.

150. *Chicano Manifesto,* ed. cit., p. 336.

151. See, for example, *The University of Chicago Spanish Dictionary,* comp. Carlos Castillo and Otto F. Bond. 2nd ed. (Chicago: Univ. of Chicago Press, 1972).

152. See John Shockley, *Chicano Revolt in a Texas Town* (Notre Dame, Ind.: Univ. of Notre Dame Press, 1974), for the history of *La Raza Unida.*

153. (New York: Praeger, 1988), pp. 41-3.

154. Barrera, p. 62.

155. Barrera, p. 51.

156. Barrera, p. 158.

157. *Culture and Democracy in the United States* (New York: Boni and Liveright, 1924), p. 108.

158. *Ibid.,* p. 119.

159. Barrera, p. 159.

160. Barrera, p. 160.

161. Barrera, p. 162.

162. Barrera, pp. 162-3.

163. Hurst Hannum and Richard Lillich, "The Concept of Autonomy in International Law," *The American Journal of International Law,* 74(4)(Oct. 1980):886-7.

164. Barrera, p. 163.

165. Barrera, p. 164.

166. Barrera, p. 171.

167. Barrera, p. 172.

168. See Linda Chavez, *Out of the Barrio: Toward a New Politics of Hispanic Assimilation* (New York: Basic Books, 1991), p. 93.

169. See Charles A. Stansfield, Jr., *New Jersey: A Geography* (Boulder, Colo.: Westview Press, 1983), p. 206.

170. See Guillermo X. Garcia, "Development of Border Urged," *[Austin] American-Statesman,* 13 Jan. 1987, Sec. A, p. 1.

171. Katherine Bishop, "California Dreaming, 1991 Version, North Secedes and Forms 51st State," *The New York Times,* 30 Nov. 1991, p. 6. For an insightful commentary on the results of the primary vote, see "A Fault-Line Shivers," *The Economist,* 13 June 1992, pp. 28-9. "The Los Angeles riots," according to this account, "may have clinched the separatist vote. In ten of the 27 disaffected counties, the yes vote was more than 70%; in the most northerly, it was more than 80%" (p. 39).

172. *The Statesman's Yearbook 1991-92,* 128th ed. (New York: St. Martin's Press, 1991), p. 272.

173. "Politics and Administration in Canada," in *The USA and Canada 1990.* 1st ed. (London: Europa Publications, 1990), p.366.

174. See Alan F. Williams and Cedric May, "Social Groupings and Regionalism in Canada," in *The USA and Canada 1990.* ed. cit., p. 393.

175. *Ibid.*

176. See Jane Jacobs, *The Question of Separatism: Quebec and the Struggle Over Sovereignty.* (New York: Random House, 1980), pp. 87-96.

177. See Kenneth McRoberts and Dale Postgate, *Quebec: Social Change and Political Crisis.* (Toronto: McClelland and Stewart, 1980), pp. 16, 47.

178. *Ibid.,* p. 52.

179. *Ibid.,* pp. 209ff.

180. David Frum, "English Canadians Get Ready to Say Goodbye to Quebec," *The Wall Street Journal,* 5 Apr. 1991, Sec. A, p. 15.

181. See William Claiborne, "Quebec's English-Speakers Looking Toward Exits," *The Washington Post,* 11 June 1991, Sec. A, p. 14. The human flight was paralleled by a flight of capital. See William Claiborne, "Political Uncertainty Affects Investment," *The Washington Post,* 18 Apr. 1990, Sec. A, p. 34.

182. Geoffrey Stevens, "After Meech Lake, Separatism Grows," *The Christian Science Monitor,* 5 Dec. 1990, p. 4.
For developments leading to and immediately following the failure of the Meech Lake Accord, see also Lewis H. Diuguid, "Separatist Movement is Resurgent in Quebec," *The Washington Post,* 10 Oct. 1989, Sec. A, p. 29; William Claiborne, "Canadian Debate on Bilingualism Fuels Unity, Charter Disputes," *The Washington*

*Post,* 20 Mar. 1990, Sec. A, p. 21; William Claiborne, "Newfoundland Balks at Move to Assuage Quebec," *The Washington Post,* 23 Mar. 1990, Sec. A, p. 16; Peter Brimelow, "Bilingualism Brouhaha in Canada," *National Review,* 16 Apr. 1991, p. 20; Andy Stark, "Canada's Constitutional Crisis: Tongue Tied," *The New Republic,* 23 Apr. 1990, pp. 16-19; William Claiborne, "Canada Faces Resurgence of Separatism," *The Washington Post,* 23 Apr. 1990, Sec. A, p. 1; Louise Lief, "A House in Two Parts: The Idea of Canada Defies Translation," *U.S. News & World Report,* 18 June 1990, pp. 29-31; David R. Francis, "Why One Canadian Province Quarrels With the Rest," *The Christian Science Monitor,* 21 June 1990, p. 10.

A useful summary of developments through 1992 is Maurice Pinard, "The Dramatic Reemergence of the Quebec Independence Movement," *Journal of International Affairs,* 45(Winter 1992): 471-497.

183. See Anthony Wilson-Smith, "Today's Man," *Maclean's,* 1 Nov. 1993, pp. 10f.

184. See William Claiborne, "Quebec Sovereignty: What Would Become of Canada?" *The Washington Post,* 28 Dec. 1990, Sec. A, p. 27.

185. See B.J. Cutler, "Another Nudge for Two Canadas," *The Washington Times,* 5 Feb. 1991, Sec. G, p. 3.

186. For a comprehensive treatment of Western Canadian separatism, see *Western Separatism: The Myths, Realities & Dangers,* eds. Larry Pratt and Garth Stevenson (Edmonton, Alta.: Hurtig, 1981).

187. See David B. Knight, "The Dilemma of Nations in a Rigid State Structured World," in *Pluralism and Political Geography: People, Territory, and State,* ed. Nurit Kliot and Stanley Waterman (London: Croom Helm, 1983), p. 122.

188. Knight, *op. cit.,* p. 123.

189. *Ibid.*

190. See John F. Burns, "Accord to Give the Eskimos Control of a Fifth of Canada," *The New York Times,* 17 Dec. 1991, Sec. A, p. 1.

191. See Barry Came *et al.,* "Drawing Lines in the Sand," *Maclean's,* 25 Nov. 1991, p. 22.

192. *Ibid.*

193. *Ibid.,* p. 23.

194. *Ibid.,* p. 24.

195. "Swiss Protest Diversity of Language," *The Arkansas Gazette,* 14 Jan. 1983, Sec. A, p. 14.

196. *Ibid.*

197. "Nationalism," in *Dictionary of the History of Ideas,* ed. Philip P. Wiener. (New York: Scribner's, 1973), III, 329.

198. (Chapel Hill: Univ. of North Carolina Press, 1974).

199. Lijphart is cited in Steiner, *op cit.,* p. 256.

200. Kohn, III, 338. For the background to the Jura separatist movement, see Johnathan Steinberg, *Why Switzerland?* (Cambridge: Cambridge Univ. Press, 1976), pp. 66-67.

201. (New York: Elsevier, 1976), p. 107.

202. *The Statesman's Yearbook 1991-1992.* (New York: St. Martin's Press, 1991), p. 193.

203. "Modernization and Ethnic Conflict in Belgium," *Political Studies,* Mar. 1979, p. 23.

204. Two fascist irredentist movements during the 1930s sought reunion of the Flemings with the Netherlands. See Otto-Ernst Schueddekopf, *Fascism* (New York: Praeger, 1973), pp. 69,73.

205. *The Statesman's Yearbook 1983-1984.* (New York: St. Martin's Press, 1983), p. 204.

206. "Count to Five and Devolve," *The Economist,* 22 July 1978, p. 39.

207. *Ibid.* See also "Limited Autonomy is Given to Regions in Belgium," *The New York Times,* 8 Aug. 1980, Sec. A, p. 9; "First Walloon Assembly is Installed by Belgians," *The New York Times,* 16 Oct. 1980, Sec. A, p. 10; *Conflict and Coexistence in Belgium: The Dynamics of a Culturally Divided Society,* ed. Arend Lijphart. (Berkeley: Univ. of California Press, 1981).

208. See Paul L. Montgomery, "Rightist and Ecology Parties Gain in Belgian Vote," *The New York Times,* 25 Nov. 1991.

209. "Belgium: A State Divided," *The World Today,* 36(1980): 223.

210. *Plagues and Peoples.* (Garden City, N.Y.: Anchor Doubleday, 1976), p. 57.

211. trans. Stephen Hardman. (New York: Praeger, 1971), p. 322.

212. Francis, *op. cit.*, p. 97.

213. *Ibid.*, p. 99.

214. *A Study of History,* Abridgement of Volumes I-VI by D.C. Somervell, (New York: Oxford Univ. Pr., 1947), I, 120.

215. "Austria-Hungary, Turkey, and the Balkans," in *The New Cambridge Modern History,* ed. F.H. Hinsley, (Cambridge Univ. Pr., 1962), XI, 339.
The Austro-Hungarian Empire was not the first to be fatally weakened by an influx of unassimilated aliens. See note 373 below.

216. See Jonathan C. Randal, "Prague Name-Changing Feud Stirs Slovak Nationalism," *The Washington Post,* 5 Apr. 1990, Sec. A, p. 39.

217. See "Slovak Lawmakers Reject Federation Pact," *Facts on File,* 2 Apr. 1992, p. 237. See also, "Check, O Slovakia," *The Economist,* 27 June 1992, p. 55; "Czechs, Slovaks ring out old federation in peace, nostalgia," *Arkansas Democrat-Gazette,* 1 Jan. 1993, Sec. A, p. 1.

218. U.S. Central Intelligence Agency, *Atlas of Eastern Europe: August 1990* (Washington, D.C.: The Agency, 1990), p. 6.

219. *Ibid.*

220. For an account of the Hungarian-Romanian conflict in Romania, see Mary Battiata, "A Clash of Cultures in Romanian Province," *The Washington Post,* 28 Mar. 1990, Sec. A, p. 17. For background information on the plight of the Gypsies, see Francine S. Kiefer, "Gypsy Asylum Seekers Test W. German Welcome," *The Christian Science Monitor,* 16 Aug. 1990, p. 5.

221. *Atlas of Eastern Europe,* p. 6.

222. See Thomas Goltz, "Exodus of Ethnic Turks Jars Bulgaria's Economy," *The Washington Post,* 12 July 1989, Sec. A, p. 17; Roland Flamini, "A Modern Balkan Exodus," *Time,* 14 Aug. 1989, p. 39.

223. "Yugoslavia Without Yugoslavs: The Roots of the Crisis," *International Affairs,* 67(1991): 253.

224. *Atlas of Eastern Europe,* p. 6.

225. Lendvai, *loc. cit.*

226. Tomislav Sunic, "The Fallacy of the Multiethnic State: The Case of Yugoslavia," *Conservative Review*, 1(Feb. 1990): 9.

227. Dennison Rusinow, "Yugoslavia: Balkan Breakup?" *Foreign Policy*, Summer 1991, p. 145.

228. (Boulder, Colo.: Westview Pr., 1992).

229. See Rusinow, p. 148.

230. See George J. Church, "Splinter, Splinter Little State," *Time*, 6 July 1992, p. 36. See also "Coming to Pieces?" *The Economist*, 14 Mar. 1992, pp. 59-60.

231. Angus Roxburgh, "Russia's Forgotten Race Faces Extinction," *The Times*, 7 May 1989.

232. See, for a typical British reaction to this development, Leo Muray, "Again -- a German Problem," *Contemporary Review*, Jan. 1992, p. 8.

233. John Kifner, "Fondness for Germany Endures in Polish Silesia," *The New York Times*, 9 Mar. 1990, Sec. A, p. 10. For an account of the resurgence of violent nationalism within Germany, see Stephen Kinzer, "German Unrest Expected to Bring Tightening of Law on Immigrants," *The New York Times*, 2 Sept. 1992, Sec. A, p. 1.

234. See Muray, p. 11.

235. "Ashes, Ashes . . . Central Europe After Forty Years," *Daedalus*, 121(2) (Spr. 1992): 214.

236. Robert J. Barro, "Small Is Beautiful," *The Wall Street Journal*, 11 Oct. 1991, Sec. A, p. 8.

237. "This Economy Won't Walk," *Newsweek*, 12 Oct. 1992, p.65.

238. *Considerations on Representative Government* (New York: Liberal Arts Pr., 1958), p. 230.

239. Without making reference to Mill, Corrado Gini, a sociologist writing in Italy in 1937, reaffirmed his basic concepts. In his essay "Authority and the Individual During the Different States of the Evolution of Nations," published in *Authority and the Individual* (Cambridge, Mass.: Harvard Univ. Pr., 1987), Gini gives greater emphasis, if anything, to the desirability of maintaining ethnic homogeneity in the state:

Homogeneity of physical characteristics, interests and feelings, which leads to reciprocal sympathy and conformity in behavior, or mutual tolerance, which smoothes out the existing differences, permits the spontaneous realization of social consensus. But this cannot be attained without the pressure of authority if the people are heterogeneous in respect to race or social position, with contrasting interests and divergent feelings, and moreover, uncompromising (p. 254).

240. *The Center Magazine,* July/Aug. 1974, p. 27.

241. *Ethnopolitics: A Conceptual Framework* (New York: Columbia Univ. Pr., 1981), p. 3.

242. "Dilemmas of Pluralism in the United States," in *Pluralism and Political Geography: People, Territory, and State,* eds. Nurit Kliat and Stanley Waterman, (London: Croom Helm, 1983), pp. 73-4.

243. *Democracy in Plural Societies: A Comparative Exploration* (New Haven, Conn.: Yale Univ. Pr., 1977), p. 4.

244. *Ibid.,* p. 25.

245. *Ibid.,* p. 16.

246. *Ibid.,* p. 106.

247. *Ibid.,* p. 100.

248. Seymour Martin Lipset, *Political Man* (Garden City, N.Y.: Doubleday, 1960), p. 92.

249. Lijphart, p. 153.

250. *Ibid.,* p. 140.

251. "Nationalism and National Minorities in East and Central Europe," *Journal of International Affairs,* 45(1)(Summer 1991): 63.

252. Schoepflin, p. 63.

253. "Land, Energy, and Water: The Constraints Governing Ideal U.S. Population Size," in *Elephants in the Volkswagen: Facing the Tough Questions About Our Overcrowded Country,* ed. Lindsey Grant (New York: W.H. Freeman, 1992), p. 23.

254. *Ibid.,* p. 30.

255. *Ibid.,* p. 25.

256. "Energy and Population: Transitional Issues and Eventual Limits," in *Elephants in the Volkswagen,* ed. cit., p. 34.

257. "Political Confrontation with Economic Reality: Mass Immigration in the Post-Industrial Age," in *Elephants in the Volkswagen,* ed. cit., p. 83.

258. *Ibid.,* pp. 79-80.

259. "On the Political Consequences of Scarcity and Economic Decline," *International Studies Quarterly,* 19(1985): 53.

260. *Ibid.,* p. 54.

261. *Ibid.,* pp. 58-59.

262. *Ibid.,* p. 60.

263. *Ibid.,* pp. 61-62.

264. *Ibid.,* pp. 59-60, 67-68.

265. See Craig R. Whitney, "Scots March to Instruct Europe on a Concept: Independence," *The New York Times* 13 Dec. 1992, Sec. 1, p. 26.

266. Gurr, *op. cit.* p. 64.

267. *Ibid.,* pp. 65-66.

268. Thomas F. Homer-Dixon, Jeffrey H. Boutwell, and George W. Rathjens, "Environmental Change and Violent Conflict," *Scientific American,* Feb. 1993, p. 38. Albert Gore, in his *Earth in the Balance* (Boston: Houghton, Mifflin, 1992) reports that "In 1989, the Iowa National Guard was called out to deliver water supplies during the drought" (p. 111).

269. See Tim Bovee, 'Census Sees Radical Shifts in U.S. Racial, Ethnic Mix," *The Birmingham News,* 29 Sept. 1993.

270. 81(May 1976): 1265-1286.

271. *Ibid.,* p. 1265.

272. p. 1266.

273. p. 1267. Schooler's authority for this statement is Gwatkin and Whitney in the 1957 edition of the *Encyclopaedia Britannica.*

274. *Ibid.*

275. *Ibid.*

276. p. 1272.

277. p. 1273.

278. pp. 1274-1281.

279. p. 1277.

280. pp. 1274-1275.

281. p. 1281.

282. 80(July 1974): 170-204.

283. p. 170.

284. Greeley, p. 175.

285. *Ibid.*, pp. 172-173.

286. p. 175.

287. p. 183.

288. p. 182.

289. p. 189.

290. See Edward R. Kantowicz, ''Politics,'' in *Harvard Encyclopedia of American Ethnic Groups,* ed. Stephan Thernstrom, (Cambridge, Mass.: Harvard Univ. Pr., 1980), pp. 807-811.

291. (New York: Free Press, 1983), p. 185.

292. For the history of American nativism, see John Higham, *Strangers in the Land: Patterns of American Nativism 1860-1925* (New York: Atheneum, 1972).

293. Susan Olzak, *The Dynamics of Ethnic Competition and Conflict* (Stanford, Calif.: Stanford Univ. Pr., 1992), p. vii.

294. *Ibid.*, p. 209.

295. *Ibid.*, pp. 221-222.

296. G.W.F. Hegel, *The Philosophy of History,* trans., J.Sibree, (New York: Dover, 1956), p. 86.

297. Huxley is quoted in William Irvine, *Apes, Angels & Victorians: A Joint Biography of Darwin & Huxley* (London: Weidenfeld & Nicolson, 1956), p. 229.

298. (New Haven, Conn.: Yale Univ. Pr., 1957).

299. See George Fields, ''Racism is Accepted Practice in Japan,'' *The Wall Street Journal,* 10 Nov. 1986, p. 23.

300. Nathan Glazer, ''Jewish Loyalties,'' *The Wilson Quarterly,* Autumn, 1981, p. 134.

301. For evidence of the racism of Hume, Kant, and Voltaire, see Leon Poliakov, *The Aryan Myth: A History of Racist and Nationalist Ideas in Europe,* trans., Edmund Howard, (London: Chatto-Heinemann, 1974), pp. 172-177.

302. See Benjamin Franklin, *Writings,* ed. J.A. Leo Lemay (New York: Library of America, 1987), pp. 374, 445-446, 710.

303. See *The Writings of Thomas Paine,* ed. Moncure Conway (1894; rpt. New York: AMS Pr., 1967), I, 87.

304. *Notes on Virginia* in *The Life and Selected Writings of Thomas Jefferson,* eds. Adrienne Koch and William Peden (New York: Modern Library, 1944), pp. 217-218.

305. See *The Federalist,* ed. Jacob E. Cooke, (Middlebury, Conn.: Wesleyan Univ. Pr., 1961), p. 9.

306. (New York: Paragon House, 1990), p. 234.

307. (Oxford: Basil Blackwell, 1986), pp. 21f.

308. The emphasis is Nillsson's. See his ''States and 'Nation-Groups': A Global Taxonomy'' in *New Nationalisms of the Developed West: Toward Explanation,* eds. Edward A. Tiryakian and Ronald Rogowski (Boston: Allen & Unwin, 1985), pp. 27-28.

309. Nillsson, *op. cit.,* pp. 28, 54.

310. Will Herberg, *Protestant-Catholic-Jew* (New York: Doubleday, 1955), p. 34.

311. John Higham, *Send These to Me: Immigrants in Urban America* (Baltimore: Johns Hopkins Univ. Pr., 1984), p. 13.

312. See "Push for Hawaii Sovereignty Grows," *The New York Times,* 18 Jan. 1993, Sec. A, p. 11.

313. For the Alaskan gubernatorial election results, see *Facts on File,* 9 Nov. 1990, p. 833.

314. See Richard N. Ostling, "Americans Facing Toward Mecca," *Newsweek,* 23 May 1988, pp. 49-50; Ari L. Goldman, "Mainstream Islam Rapidly Embraced By Black Americans," *The New York Times,* 20 Feb. 1989, pp. 1, 6.

315. See Wilferd Madelung, "Imamate." in *Encyclopedia of Religion,* ed. Mircea Eliade, (New York: Macmillan, 1987), VII, 114-119.

316. See, for example, Sonia L. Nazario, "Sacrificing Roosters to Glorify the Gods Has Miami in a Snit," *The Wall Street Journal,* 18 Oct. 1984, p. 1; Carlos Sanchez, "Animal Sacrifice Ritual Spurs Rights Debate in D.C.," *The Washington Post,* 30 Nov. 1987, Sec. C, p. 1; Rick Mitchell, "Power of the Orishas," *Los Angeles Times Magazine,* 7 Feb. 1988, pp. 16-18, 21, 30, 32; David Kocieniewski, "Voodoo Tale Doesn't Sway Judge in Narcotics Case," *The Detroit News,* 20 Apr. 1989, Sec. B, p. 6.
For a popular journalistic account of the heinous crimes (human sacrifice and cannibalism) committed by a group of Santeria cultists who preyed upon the inhabitants of a Texas border city, see Clifford L. Linedecker, *Hell Ranch: Nightmare of Voodoo, Drugs and Death in Matamoros* (New York: Tom Doherty Associates, 1990). See also Peter Applebome, "Drugs, Death and the Occult Meet in Grisly Inquiry at Mexico Border," *The New York Times,* 12 Apr. 1989, p. 1; Richard Woodbury, "Cult of the Red-Haired Devil," *Time,* 24 Apr. 1989, p. 30; Phil Davison, "Concern Voiced on Spread of Devil Worship in Mexico," *The San Diego Union,* 12 May 1989, Sec. A, p. 25; Phil Davison, "Mexican Celebrities Linked to the 'Satanic Godfather'," *The Washington Times,* 12 May 1989, Sec. A, p. 1.

317. Renan is quoted by Louis L. Snyder in his *Encyclopedia of Nationalism,* ed. cit., p. 232.

318. (New York: Elsevier, 1976), p. 78.

319. Barth's definition is thus paraphrased by Hoyt S. Alvarson in his "The Roots of Time: A Comment on Utilitarian and Primordial Sentiments in Ethnic Identification," in *Ethnic Autonomy: Comparative Dynamics,* ed. Raymond L. Hall (New York: Pergamon Pr., 1979), p. 13.

320. John R. Baker, *Race* (New York: Oxford Univ. Pr., 1974), p. 4.

321. A useful definition of the concept of nature and its relation to humanity is John Stuart Mill's "Nature," published in 1874. See, among other editions, *Nature, and the Utility of Religion*, ed. George Nahknikian (New York: Liberal Arts Pr., 1958).

322. The following are among the better-known works by these ethologists: Jane Goodall, *In the Shadow of Man* (1971); Konrad Lorenz, *On Aggression* (1966); Desmond Morris, *The Naked Ape* (1967), *The Human Zoo* (1969); Lionel Tiger and Robin Fox, *The Imperial Animal* (1971). Robert Ardrey, although not a scientist, is worthy of mention for his works *The Social Contract* (1970) and *The Territorial Imperative* (1966).

323. *Sociobiology: The New Synthesis* (Cambridge, Mass.: Harvard Univ. Pr., 1975), p. 4.

324. *Ibid.*, pp. 9-10.

325. *The Human Zoo* (New York: McGraw-Hill, 1969), p. 136.

326. *Sociobiology*, ed. cit., p. 565.

327. *Ethnic Groups in Conflict* (Berkeley: Univ. of California Pr., 1985), pp. 143-144.

328. "Introduction by the Editors," in *The Sociobiology of Ethnocentrism: Evolutionary Dimensions of Xenophobia, Discrimination, Racism and Nationalism*, eds. V. Reynolds, Vincent S.E. Falger, and Ian Vine (Athens: Univ. of Georgia Pr.), pp.xvii-xviii.

329. "Inclusive Fitness and Ethnocentrism," in *The Sociobiology of Ethnocentrism*, p. 112.

330. "Genetic Similarity as a Mediator of Interpersonal Relationships," in *The Sociobiology of Ethnocentrism*, p. 130.

331. "A Study in the Evolution of Ethnocentrism," in *The Sociobiology of Ethnocentrism*, p. 154.

332. "Biological Bases of Social Prejudices," in *The Sociobiology of Ethnocentrism*, pp. 192-193.

333. *Ibid.*, p. 195.

334. *Ibid.*, pp. 198-199.

335. "Group Identification and Political Socialisation," in *The Sociobiology of Ethnocentrism*, p. 189.

336. *Sociobiology*, ed. cit., p. 573.

337. For a review of Hall's *Mammals of North America,* see *Guide to Reference Books,* ed. Eugene P. Sheehy, 10th ed., (Chicago: American Library Association, 1986), p. 1180.

338. Hall's article was originally published in 1960 in *Mankind Quarterly.* For the paragraphs quoted here, see the pamphlet edition, *Zoological Subspecies of Man* (New York: I.A.A.E.E., 1960), pp. 3-4.

Hall emphasizes, in the following, that subspecies of humans are determined by the same criteria as are subspecies of other mammals:

> Something that most non-zoologists seem not to know is that the subspecies of man are distinguished one from the other by the same sort of differences -- characters, in zoological parlance -- as are subspecies of almost any other kind of mammal, say, subspecies of the mole, marmoset, or moose. For example, in the skull of a Point Barrow Eskimo, one of the races of the subspecies *Homo sapiens asiaticus,* the size and shape of the bony opening for the nose is significantly different from that in a Zulu Negro, one of the races of the subspecies *Homo sapiens afer.* In the Eskimo the opening is narrow (less than half as wide as high), whereas in the Negro it is wide -- more than half as wide as high. Under a microscope the hair of the head of the Zulu is seen to have a characteristic shape in cross section, and inspection by means of only the naked eye reveals that the hair of the Zulu is kinky and his skin black, whereas the Eskimo's hair is straight and his skin yellow or dark reddish. Even cursory comparison will serve to multiply this list of differences. Similarly, in the moose, the subspecies *Alces alces alces* of Europe has the premaxillary bone extended back beneath the nasal bone and the color of its hair is grayish, whereas the subspecies *Alces alces gigas* from Alaska differs in that the premaxillary bone does not extend back so far as the nasal bone and the hair is blackish . . . . (pp. 1-2)

339. *Ibid.,* pp. 4, 6.

340. *Ibid.,* p. 2.

341. It is the thesis of Peter Zwick, argued in his *National Communism* (Boulder, Colo.: Westview Pr., 1983) that "from its very conception communism has been national and that the term 'international communism' has been badly misinterpreted by communists and noncommunists alike" (p. 13). According to Zwick's account (on pp. 59-64), Stalin sought to defend the hegemony of Russia over other nationalities in the USSR by arguing that the location of most of the industrial proletariat in Russia gave it a role of leadership as a nation.

342. Samuel P. Oliner, "Union of Soviet Socialist Republics," in *The International Handbook on Race and Race Relations,* ed. Jay A. Singer, (New York: Greenwood Pr., 1987), p. 340.

343. *Ibid.,* p. 23. Rockett's book was published by Praeger at New York in 1981.

344. Teresa Rakowska-Harmstone, "Chickens Coming Home to Roost: A Perspective on Soviet Ethnic Relations," *Journal of International Affairs,* 45(Winter 1992): 545.

345. *Ibid.,* pp. 539-540.

346. *Distant Neighbors: A Portrait of the Mexicans* (New York: Knopf, 1985), p. 279-280.

347. *Ibid.,* p. 199.

348. *Ibid.,* p. 200. On the same page, Riding notes that "During the 1910 Revolution, Indians once again provided most of the combatants and casualties. In many areas, they were not ever sure why they were fighting; decisions would be made in their name, but they would not be consulted."

349. For the history of racist thought among the Brazilian elite, see Thomas E. Skidmore, *Black Into White: Race and Nationality in Brazilian Thought* (New York: Oxford Univ. Pr., 1974). Pages 7, 39-40 refer to the UNESCO study.

350. *Race, Class, and Power in Brazil,* ed. Pierre-Michel Fontaine, (Los Angeles: Center for Afro-American Studies, Univ. of California Pr., 1985), pp. 39-40.

351. *Ibid.,* p. 42.

352. *Ibid.,* p. 54.

353. *Ibid.,* p. 7.

354. Anani Dzidzienyo, "Brazil," in *International Handbook on Race and Race Relations,* ed. cit., p. 25.

355. See James Brooke, "Brazil's Idol Is a Blonde, and Some Ask 'Why?'," *The New York Times,* 31 July 1990, Sec. A, p. 4.

356. *Ibid.*

357. See James Brooke, "White Flight in Brazil? Secession Caldron Boils," *The New York Times,* 12 May 1993, Sec. A, p. 6.

358. See Nathaniel C. Nash, "Uruguay Is on Notice: Blacks Ask Recognition," *The New York Times,* 7 May 1993, Sec. A, p. 4.

359. *America South* (Philadelphia: Lippincott, 1938), pp. 52-53.

360. *Ibid.,* p. 53.

361. *Latin America: Essays in Continuity and Change,* ed. Harold Blakemore, (London: BBC, 1974), p. 66. For a description of the persistence of subspecies endogamy in northeast Brazil, see L.L. Cavalli-Sforza and W.F. Bodmer, *The Genetics of Human Populations* (San Francisco: W.H. Freeman, 1974), pp. 788-789.

362. Herman E. Daly, "Ultimate Confusion: The Economics of Julian Simon," *Futures,* 17(Oct. 1986): 446.

363. *Ibid.,* p. 447.

364. *Ibid.,* p. 448.

365. *Ibid.,* p. 449.

366. Francis Fukuyama, "Immigrants and Family Values," *Commentary,* May 1993, pp. 31-32.

367. Jeane Kirkpatrick, "We Need the Immigrants," *The Los Angeles Times,* 30 June 1986, Sec. A.

368. Tom Bethell, "What Immigration Crisis?" *The American Spectator,* Aug. 1984, p. 9.

369. See U.S. Cong., Senate, Committee on the Judiciary, Subcommittee on Immigration, *Hearings on Immigration Reform Act of 1965,* Feb. 10, 1965 to Mar. 11, 1965, (Washington, D.C.: GPO, 1965), pp. 216-217, 118-120. For similar testimony, see pp. 8, 11, 20, 29, 62-63, 66-67, 71, 108, 136, 224, 681-683.

370. For one of the most insightful studies of the New Left, see Stanley Rothman and S. Robert Lichter, *Roots of Radicalism: Jews, Christians, and the New Left.* (New York, Oxford Univ. Pr., 1982).

371. Edward Abbey, "Immigration and Liberal Taboos," in *One Life at a Time, Please* (New York: Henry Holt and Company, 1988), p. 43. Abbey's account of his trials in getting this essay published appears on pp. 1-3.

372. *Around the Cragged Hill* (New York: W.W. Norton, 1993), p. 154.

373. See Edward Gibbon, *History of the Decline and Fall of the Roman Empire* (New York: Modern Library, n.d.), I, 956. The account of the settlement of the Goths in the empire occupies the closing pages of chapter XXVI. The Goths, fleeing an onslaught of the Huns, had sought permission to settle south of the Danube. In 376 A.D., the emperor Theodosius gave permission for the Goths to settle in that area of the empire in exchange for their swearing of fealty to Rome and their provision of 40,000 troops to be in the service of the empire of the East (I, 953).

374. According to the following account given by Gibbon, the emperor and his party were confident that the Goths could somehow be assimilated as loyal subjects of the empire:

> The advocates of Theodosius could affirm, with some appearance of truth and reason, that it was impossible to extirpate so many warlike tribes, who were rendered desperate by the loss of their native country; and that the exhausted provinces would be revived by a fresh supply of soldiers and husbandmen. The barbarians still wore an angry and hostile aspect; but the experience of past times might encourage the hope that they would acquire the habits of industry and obedience; that their manners would be polished by time, education, and the influence of Christianity; and that their posterity would insensibly blend with the great body of the Roman people . . . . Notwithstanding these specious arguments and these sanguine expectations, it was apparent to every discerning eye that the Goths would long remain the enemies, and might soon become the conquerors of the Roman empire (I, 954).

Gibbon, of course, does not use the terms, but it is evident that the Romans assumed that behavioral assimilation would prove to be as good as structural assimilation.

Under Arcadius, son of Theodosius and emperor of the East, "a plan was judiciously conceived, which, in the space of seven years, would have secured the command of the Danube, by establishing on that river a perpetual fleet of two hundred and fifty armed vessels" (II. 216). However, by then it was too late for Rome to reassert control of its borders. Soon after the death of Theodosius, the Goths revolted and overran Greece. (See chapter XXX of Gibbon.) During the period from 408 to 449 A.D., the Goths thrice besieged Rome, and pillaged the city once. While the Goths ravaged Italy and made incursions into Gaul and Spain, the island of Britain was abandoned by the over-extended Romans. (See chapter XXXI.)

Following the Goths came the Huns and the Vandals. (See chapters XXXIV and XXXV.) They were, of course, unwelcome invaders from the start. While the Romans could rationalize their weakness in admitting the Goths, many of whom were already converts to Arian Christianity, as an accession of new subjects to the empire, they could entertain no such illusions regarding the much more alien Huns.

375. See Garrett Hardin, "The P's and Q's of Immigration: A Letter to My Granddaughter," *Chronicles*, June 1993, pp. 16-18. Hardin has also published *Living Within Limits: Ecology, Economics, and Population Taboos* (New York: Oxford Univ. Pr., 1993).

376. It may, at first thought, seem unlikely that the various European nationality groups will be geographically distributed as described. However, seventy years after Horace M. Kallen described this pattern, it still prevailed, as the 1980 and 1990 censuses have revealed. See the detailed maps in James P. Allen and Eugene J. Turner, *We the People: An Atlas of America's Ethnic Diversity* (New York: Macmillan, 1988).

The largest European American ethnic-geographic bloc will be German America, which, ironically, may have its political awakening long after it has lost almost all sense of its *Deutschtum*.

377. There will, of course, be other separatist models. For another example of a separatist movement driven by rancor over taxation, the Northern League of Italy, see James Sturz, "Bossi Boots," *The New Republic,* 15 Feb. 1993, pp. 15-16.

378. See, for example, Amaury de Riencourt, *The Coming Caesars* (New York: Coward-McCann, 1957).

379. John Lukacs, "The Stirrings of History: A New World Rises From the Ruins of Europe," *Harper's,* Aug. 1990, p. 48.